THE EGYPTIANS
HISTORY SOCIETY RELIGION

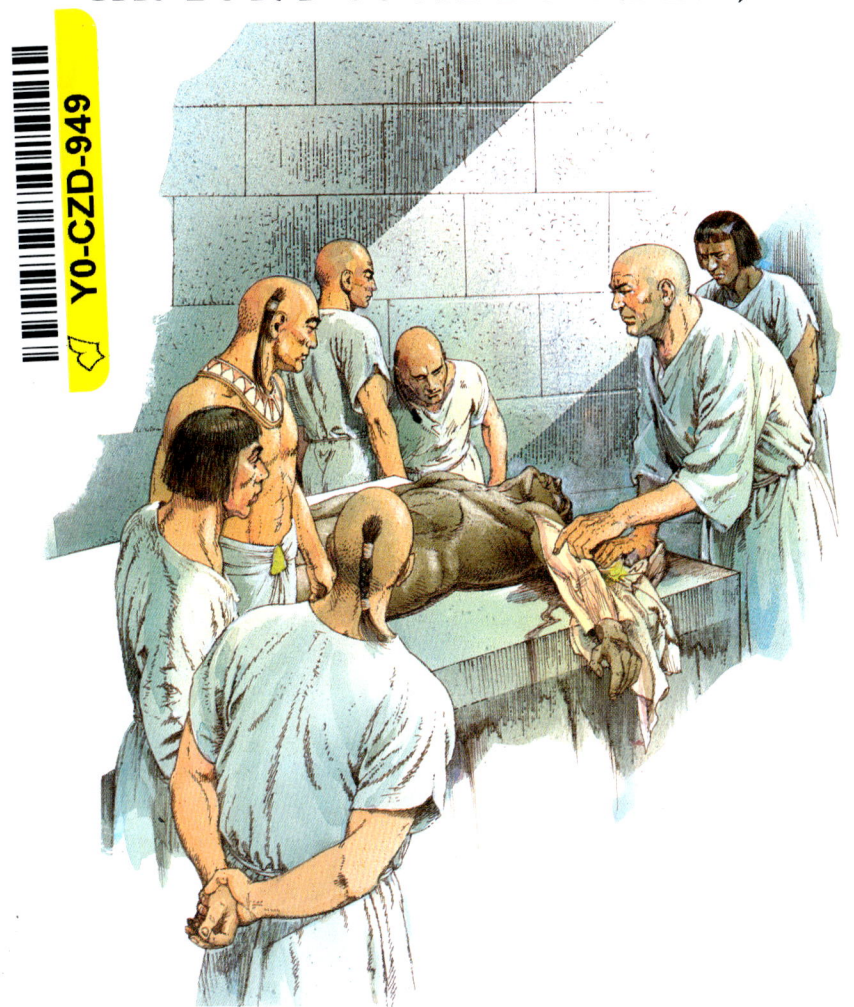

Renzo Rossi
Illustrations by:
Sergio

BARRON'S

DoGi

English translation © Copyright 1999
by Barron's Educational Series, Inc.
Original edition © 1999 by DoGi spa, Florence Italy
Title of original edition: *Gli egizi: Storia Società Religione*
Italian edition by: Renzo Rossi
Illustrations by: Sergio
Editors:
Andrea Bachini
Francesco Milo
Graphic Display: Sebastiano Ranchetti
Art director: Sebastiano Ranchetti
Page make-up:
Katherine Carlson Forden
 Sebastiano Ranchetti
Iconographic researcher: Katherine Carlson Forden

English translation by Anna Maria Salmeri Pherson

All rights reserved. No part of this book may be
reproduced in any form, by photostat,
microfilm, xerography, or any other means or
incorporated into any information retrieval
system, electronic or mechanical, without the written
permission of the copyright owner.

All inquiries should be addressed to:
Barron's Educational Series, Inc.
250 Wireless Boulevard
Hauppauge, NY 11788
http://www.barronseduc.com

Library of Congress Catalog Card No. 98-76187

International Standard Book No. 0-7641-0942-1

Printed in Italy
9 8 7 6 5 4 3 2 1

Table of Contents

- 4   The Discovery of the Past
- 8   The Origins
- 12   The Land of the Nile
- 30   The Old Kingdom: The State
- 50   The Old Kingdom: The Religion
- 64   The First Intermediate Period
- 68   The Middle Kingdom
- 80   The Second Intermediate Period
- 84   The New Kingdom
- 114   The Decline of Egypt
- 120   Index

THE DISCOVERY OF THE PAST

The Egypt of the pharaohs, with its three thousand years of history, stone giants, original cult of the dead, political stability, and society's complex organization, has fascinated archeologists, adventurers, and travelers for all time.

One need only look to the movies to witness the lure of ancient Egypt. From the 1930s to the present, mummies, pyramids, and their mysteries have continued to be the subjects of many movies. Scholars are not the only ones who are fascinated with the Egyptian civilization; many publications have been written about it, and it has been the historical background of much literature, some of it very successful.

This great interest in Egyptian artifacts is a trend started by the ancient Romans, whose emperors had obelisks moved from Egypt to Rome. Since the end of the eighteenth century,

EGYPT FASCINATES
Each year during the past ten years, millions of people have toured Egypt. About 150 world-renowned Egyptian collections exist. Universities now teach scientific Egyptology and both literature and the movies popularize Egyptian culture.

archeologists and historians studying Egypt, known as Egyptologists, have made a vital contribution to the understanding of this ancient civilization. In 1799, in conjunction with Napoleon's military expedition to Egypt (1798–1799), soldiers discovered a stele, or stone, with a long inscription in three languages, including Greek, at Rosetta, near Alexandria. This discovery aroused enormous interest and curiosity, and made it possible to decipher the writing of the ancient Egyptians, called hieroglyphs. From this discovery, a world reappeared that had practically vanished in memory and physical presence, since the fourth century A.D.

In 391, the Roman emperor Theodosius I had decreed the closing of all pagan temples in the empire. Some cult followers in Egypt still used hieroglyphs, which they hid quickly after this edict and, in time, their meaning was forgotten. Only the descriptions of Egypt left during the Classical Age by Greek and Roman historians and travelers remained. The historian Herodotus had written an account of his trip to Egypt around 450 B.C. Later, others followed his example. The Greek geographer Strabo in 30 A.D. wrote about his trip to Egypt that was then dominated by Romans. The Greek historian, Plutarch, who lived between 46 A.D. and 125 A.D., informed the world about one of the most famous cults of ancient Egypt, that of Isis and Osiris. In the Classical Age, therefore, Egypt was visited and written about. Then, in the fourth century A.D., this activity stopped. The Arab invasion of 641 placed Egypt under Muslim rule. It became difficult for Europeans to visit it; furthermore, the hieroglyphs on the monuments were no longer understood. The travelers of the later Middle Ages (fourteenth century) and of the Renaissance (sixteenth century) ventured up to the area closest to the Mediterranean. They went no further, since for them this was only a

The father of history
The Greek Herodotus (c. 485–c. 425 B.C.) was one of the earliest travelers of the classical world to describe Egypt. His narration captivated readers, but was not very objective. He based it upon the traditions passed down by priests as well as upon often-fantastic stories from the tour guides of the epoch.

A key discovery
In 1799, during Napoleon's campaign in Egypt, French troops unearthed the Rosetta Stone.

PTOLMYS

ΠΤΟΛΕΜΑΙΟΣ
PTOLEMAIOS

From a comparison From the Greek form of the name *Ptolemy*, Champollion identified its equivalent in hieroglyphs. This information was the first step towards the interpretation of the mysterious Egyptian writing.

Rosetta Stone
It displays a decree of Ptolemy V of 196 B.C., chiseled in three forms of writing: hieroglyphs, demotic script, and Greek. The Greek served as a key to deciphering the hieroglyphs.

stop on the way to Palestine. However, a certain interest flickered because the Bible's Old Testament mentioned Egypt by virtue of the link, since the second millennium B.C., between Egypt's history and that of the Jews.

During the seventeenth and eighteenth centuries, almost the only foreigners to visit and write about Egypt were Catholic missionaries. The French baron Dominique-Vivant Denon (1747–1825) explored the country as an attaché of Napoleon's expeditionary force, brought home several Egyptian works, and wrote a treatise illustrated with sketches. His report spread, with acclaim, throughout Europe and greatly contributed to a resurgence of interest in Egypt. In France in 1813, he published his *The Description of Egypt*, a twenty-four volume work.

In 1822, the Frenchman Jean-François Champollion (1790–1832) deciphered the hieroglyphs. The mysterious inscriptions were understood and Egyptology (or the science of Egypt) was definitively recognized. Since then, many scholars have studied Egypt. Beautiful works were brought to Europe for study and display in important museums. The Frenchman Auguste Mariette (1821–1881) succeeded in putting an end to the export of Egyptian artifacts out of the country. In Cairo, he opened a museum entirely dedicated to Egypt and promoted excavations and research.

In 1922, the discovery of the tomb of Pharaoh Tutankhamen by the Englishman Howard Carter and Lord George Carnarvon is surely one of the most famous and fascinating finds of twentieth-century archeology.

THE ORIGINS

Characteristics of the Egyptian civilization appeared already at the end of the fourth millennium B.C. Language, writing, and religion took shape and planted their roots over a long period.

The populations that were to take possession of the Nile Valley and give birth to the Egyptian civilization belonged to a North African ethnic group that mingled over time with other populations from Asia.

Between 8,000 and 9,000 years ago, at the end of the last Ice Age, the northern regions of Africa looked much different than they do today. Where the Sahara desert is located was a huge, verdant savanna. Streams and lakes were filled with plants (palms, pines, and olive trees) and animals (crocodiles, antelopes, and a variety of fish), their presence recorded by many inscriptions in rock. Indeed, it was an inviting place for human settlement.

After the Ice Age, the Northern Hemisphere experienced a short period of heavy rainfall, followed by a much drier period. The lack of rain decided a new course for humans: from hunters and gatherers, people became herdsmen and tillers. By the first half of the fourth millennium, the North African savanna dried up and its population moved to the alluvial valley of the

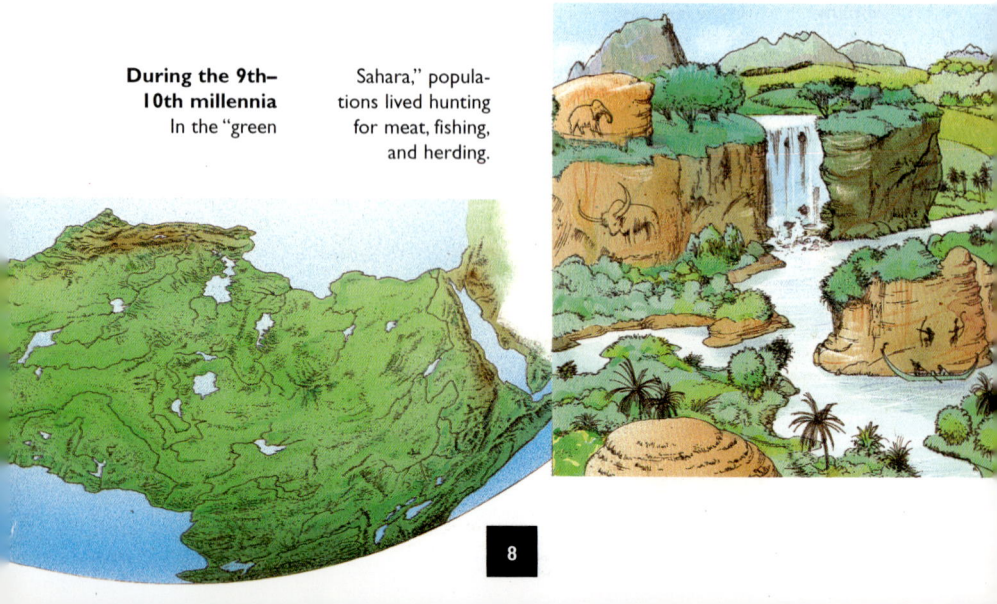

During the 9th–10th millennia In the "green Sahara," populations lived hunting for meat, fishing, and herding.

First half of the 4th millennium
The Sahara is almost completely parched. Herdsmen live only in the few humid areas.

End of the 4th millennium
The Sahara is an uninhabited desert. Its population has moved to the alluvial plain of the Nile.

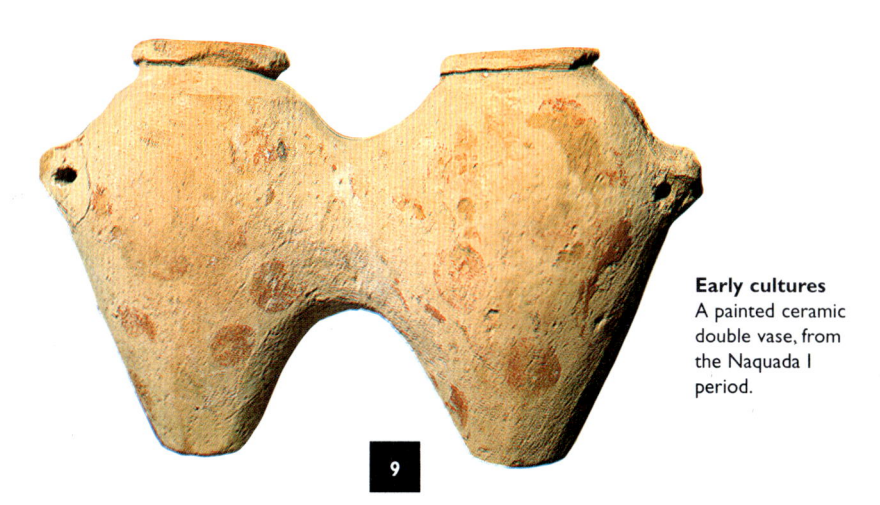

Early cultures
A painted ceramic double vase, from the Naquada I period.

Nile and to such lower areas as the Faiyum, regions that retained the annual floodwaters of the river.

The first inhabitants

The agricultural transformation of the Nile Valley required the combined efforts of communities that were larger and more organized than the original settlers.

Under the authority of the strongest agricultural center, small political communities developed; the leadership of a ruler, the predecessor of a future king, began to prevail. Speech and memory were not enough to collect and transmit all the information needed to organize the group. Thus, people began to use a form of writing to record these concepts.

In the valley, early cultures flourished: Naquada I (4000–3500 B.C.) with urban settlements in Upper Egypt, and Naquada II (3500–3300 B.C.) that extended to the Delta.

Unification of the two kingdoms

Living along the Nile demanded a steady collective effort only achievable under a central power that regulated and protected the society within the territory and acted as an intermediary with the divinity, the source of all things necessary to life. Pharaonic civilization, whose origins remain obscure, established itself in this way. The early chieftains fought among themselves to extend their power. With annexations, villages grew until, around 3200 B.C., during the Predynastic period, Egypt contained two

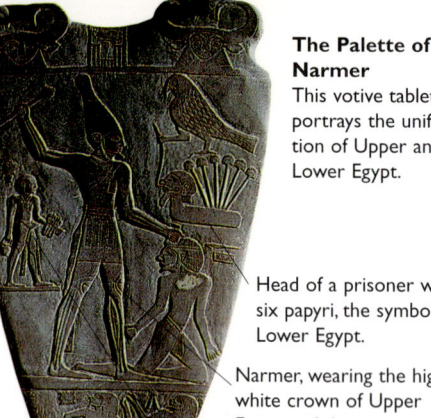

The Palette of Narmer
This votive tablet portrays the unification of Upper and Lower Egypt.

Head of a prisoner with six papyri, the symbol of Lower Egypt.

Narmer, wearing the high white crown of Upper Egypt, with his enemy kneeling before him.

One of the high officials hands the sandals to the king.

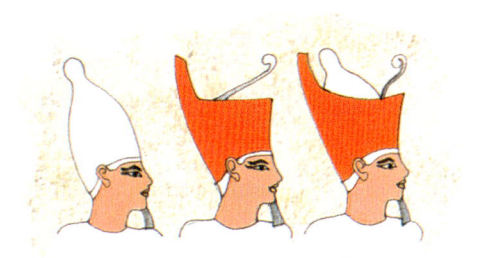

The three crowns
The double crown symbolizes Narmer's unification of Egypt into only one state: the high white crown of the South and the red crown of the North.

Stele of King Snake
Document of the 1st Dynasty showing the falcon-god, Horus, above the panel, boxing the name of the king, represented by the snake, and the façade (*serekh*) of the royal palace.

Mace of King Scorpion
The king, wearing a white crown, ritually opens a canal. He holds a hoe in his hands and stands over a dirt bearer carrying a basket.

states: Lower or Northern Egypt, which included the entire Delta, and Upper Egypt, the valley to the south. The process of unification culminated around 3000 B.C. when the king of Upper Egypt, Menes, as he is traditionally called, or Narmer, the name suggested by archeological sources, conquered the Delta. He founded the first of thirty dynasties, which ruled until the days of Alexander the Great, in the fourth century B.C. With their kingdom finally unified, the kings of the Archaic period (Early Dynastic period: First and Second Dynasties) strove to bring justice and order, personified by the goddess Ma'at. Through the Rule, all the Pharaoh's actions worked towards achieving *Ma'at* (peace, wisdom, truth, science, and harmony). The equilibrium of ancient Egypt depended on this permanent tie with Ma'at.

THE LAND OF THE NILE

In Egypt, it seldom rains. The Nile River, with its annual floods, brings water to the country. However, only hard work and careful planning ensure that agriculture prospers, because it forms the base of Egyptian civilization.

In Khartoum, in the Sudan, the river receives the waters of the White Nile, gushing from the great equatorial lakes of eastern Africa and those of the Blue Nile, swollen by the rains that fall in the distant highlands of Ethiopia. Until the nineteenth century, their combined forces caused yearly flooding. After receiving the waters of the Atbara River, the Nile describes a large loop across the parched steppes of Nubia. Then, following a series of cataracts, or steep rapids, the last one upstream of Aswan, it enters a long valley flanked by deserts, and glides lazily towards the Mediterranean. It encounters no other tributary, but only a natural canal outlet called the Bahr Yusef or Joseph's Canal, which breaks the big river at Asyut and runs parallel to it, leftward, up to the Faiyum depression. Here it branches out and disappears. The Delta begins north of Cairo, limited by the Rosetta branch in the west and by the Damietta in the east.

Timeless beauty
Egypt's everlasting elements: the river, palm groves, fields, the necropolis, the village, and, in the background, the desert.

Length
From its source to the delta, the river glides for almost 4101 miles, 600 of which are in Egyptian territory.

Width
In the Nubian region, the Nile River averages a width of 2953 ft. in the Egyptian valley.

Delta
It features an equilateral triangular shape of 118 miles per side. It splits into five main branches.

Climate
It is dry, with strong temperature shifts both within the day and during the year. Aswan records the highest temperatures in the country.

Cataracts
They are waterfalls in the riverbed. The Nile had six main and several minor cataracts.

The full flood
The level of the river rises to 23 ft. at Aswan and to 13 ft. in Cairo.

A satellite view
The Delta has been compared to the lotus flower; the Faiyum representing the leaf departing from the stem. The satellite image illustrates this image.

The fertile land
Worked fields along the riverside in the most fertile area of the valley.

The desert
The Libyan Desert, a flat and harsh expanse, broken now and then by the green of an oasis.

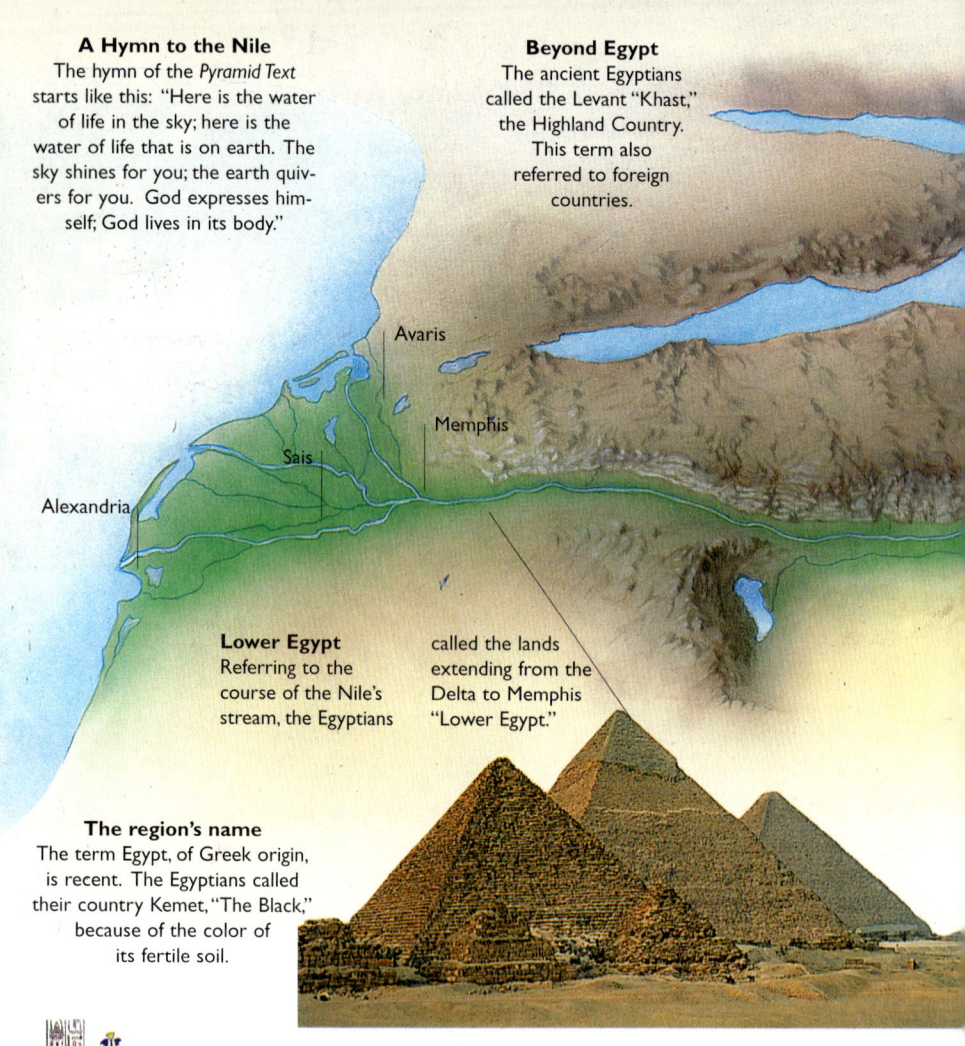

A Hymn to the Nile
The hymn of the *Pyramid Text* starts like this: "Here is the water of life in the sky; here is the water of life that is on earth. The sky shines for you; the earth quivers for you. God expresses himself; God lives in its body."

Beyond Egypt
The ancient Egyptians called the Levant "Khast," the Highland Country. This term also referred to foreign countries.

Avaris

Memphis

Sais

Alexandria

Lower Egypt
Referring to the course of the Nile's stream, the Egyptians called the lands extending from the Delta to Memphis "Lower Egypt."

The region's name
The term Egypt, of Greek origin, is recent. The Egyptians called their country Kemet, "The Black," because of the color of its fertile soil.

The Black Land and the Red Lands

Together, the Nile Valley and Delta form an area of 13,127 square miles (slightly smaller than Belgium). The ancient Egyptians call it the Black Land (*kemi*) because of the color of its soil, which contains black silt powder left behind by the flooding. The region owes its extraordinary fertility to this topsoil. The Delta forms a rich and magnificent triangular plain. Several branches cross it, heading towards the low and uniform coast of the Mediterranean.

A long swirl of earth lies south of the Delta. It is large, about 12.4 miles along the railway that separates the towns of

The sea
For many centuries, the Egyptians called the Red and the Mediterranean Seas the "big green."

Upper Egypt
It included the valley running from Memphis to the First Cataract, near Aswan.

The First Cataract, Abu Simbel

The capitals
During different periods, the capitals of ancient Egypt have been: Thinis (beginning of the Old Kingdom), Memphis (Old Kingdom), Thebes (Middle and New Kingdoms), Avaris (under the Hyksos), Sais (in the Late Ages), and Alexandria (founded and elected capital in the period following the Egypt of the pharaohs).

Cairo (Memphis) and Luxor (Thebes), and only 3.1 miles along the railway between Luxor and Aswan.

The pinnacles of the plateaus surrounding the valley rise fiercely, as high as 492–656 ft.

Beyond this area spread the Red Lands of the Libyan and Arabic deserts. The first, on the western side, is primarily flat and open, with a series of oases roughly parallel to the course of the Nile. The latter desert forms a torrid plateau crisscrossed by the deep riverbeds of old streams (*uadi*), now dried up, where few living things could survive. This area, however, harbors rich resources: mines of gold, copper, tin, and precious stones.

The gift of the Nile

Egypt would be a large desert, a Red Land itself, had the Nile not turned it into a very long oasis, inside a desert. In Egypt, thanks to its generous river, agriculture has always been paramount; the valley resembled a gigantic farm. In fact, the economies of the two Egyptian territories integrated because their inhabitants had everything to gain and nothing to lose by organizing themselves into a bigger community, one that extended from Aswan to the Mediterranean Sea. This joining of forces was the best way to exploit the floodwaters with hydraulic works and to gather extra food reserves during lean drought years. Moreover, the south needed certain products available in the north and vice versa. Natural flora, such as papyrus, lotus, water lily, reed, and acacia, covered the entire country. Farmers cultivated barley, flax, emmer, wheat, many types of vegetables, and grapes with great success. Even the many animals depended on the Nile: hippopotamus and crocodile, and also antelope, gazelle, and marsh birds (lapwings, herons, and cranes) and many types of fish.

Indeed, the Greek historian Herodotus called Egypt the "gift of the Nile." All this would have been impossible without the great full flood of the river, which the munificent gods granted to the country a prodigious and regular natural gift.

A TRIBUTE TO MANPOWER
The work of men that pleases the gods and, thanks to the Nile, makes the land prosperous. Found in the painted wall of the tomb of Sennedjem, the overseer of the necropolis (the place where dead were buried) of Thebes (1300 B.C.).

Flooding

Around each July 19, Sirius, the star of *Sothis*, appeared low on the eastern horizon. This signified to the Egyptian farmers that the full yearly flood of the Nile was coming, and they confidently awaited it. They did not consider it a catastrophe, but a divine blessing of the generous god Hapi, personification of the river. Hapi caused the river to overflow and flood the surrounding lands, leaving a layer of mud rich with the silt that gave life

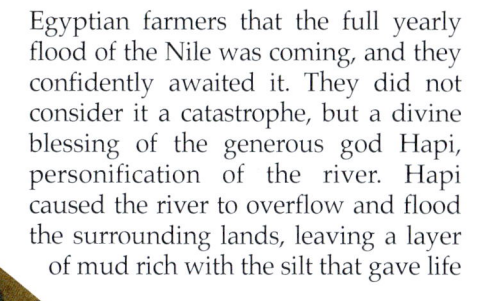

Enterprise Egypt
Especially during harvesting, the local population could not possibly do all the work. Squads of peasants formed, moving from the south (where the grain ripened earlier) to the north to supply the extra laborers.

Few trees
In Egypt, no tall trees grew for wood and no olive trees grew either, so oil was extracted from castor oil plants. The large-leafed African fan palms (used for mats), date palms, the carob tree, the fig tree, the tamarisk, and the sycamore fig grew abundantly.

and prosperity. Although necessary, the floodwaters could both harm and help farmers. When the waters churned violently, they smashed the dikes and washed away the fields. When the waters were scarce, the resulting drought might impoverish the whole country. Therefore, they had to learn to control and harness the floods by constructing adequate dams and dikes, which stored water in basins to irrigate the fields all year long. One month after the floods, when the soil was saturated, the water was collected in smaller basins and finally channeled to the Nile. An effective network of canals extended to the lands farther away from the river, which the floodwaters did not reach.

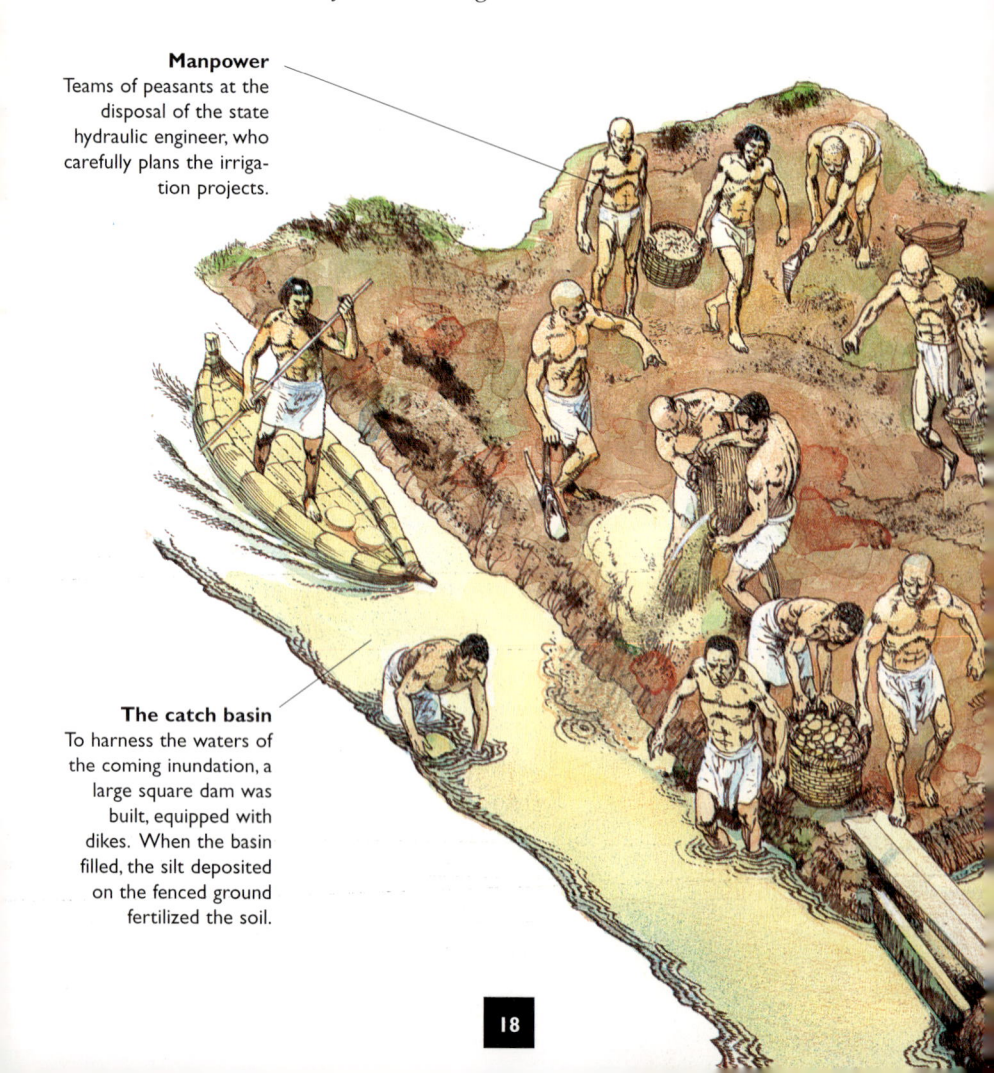

Manpower
Teams of peasants at the disposal of the state hydraulic engineer, who carefully plans the irrigation projects.

The catch basin
To harness the waters of the coming inundation, a large square dam was built, equipped with dikes. When the basin filled, the silt deposited on the fenced ground fertilized the soil.

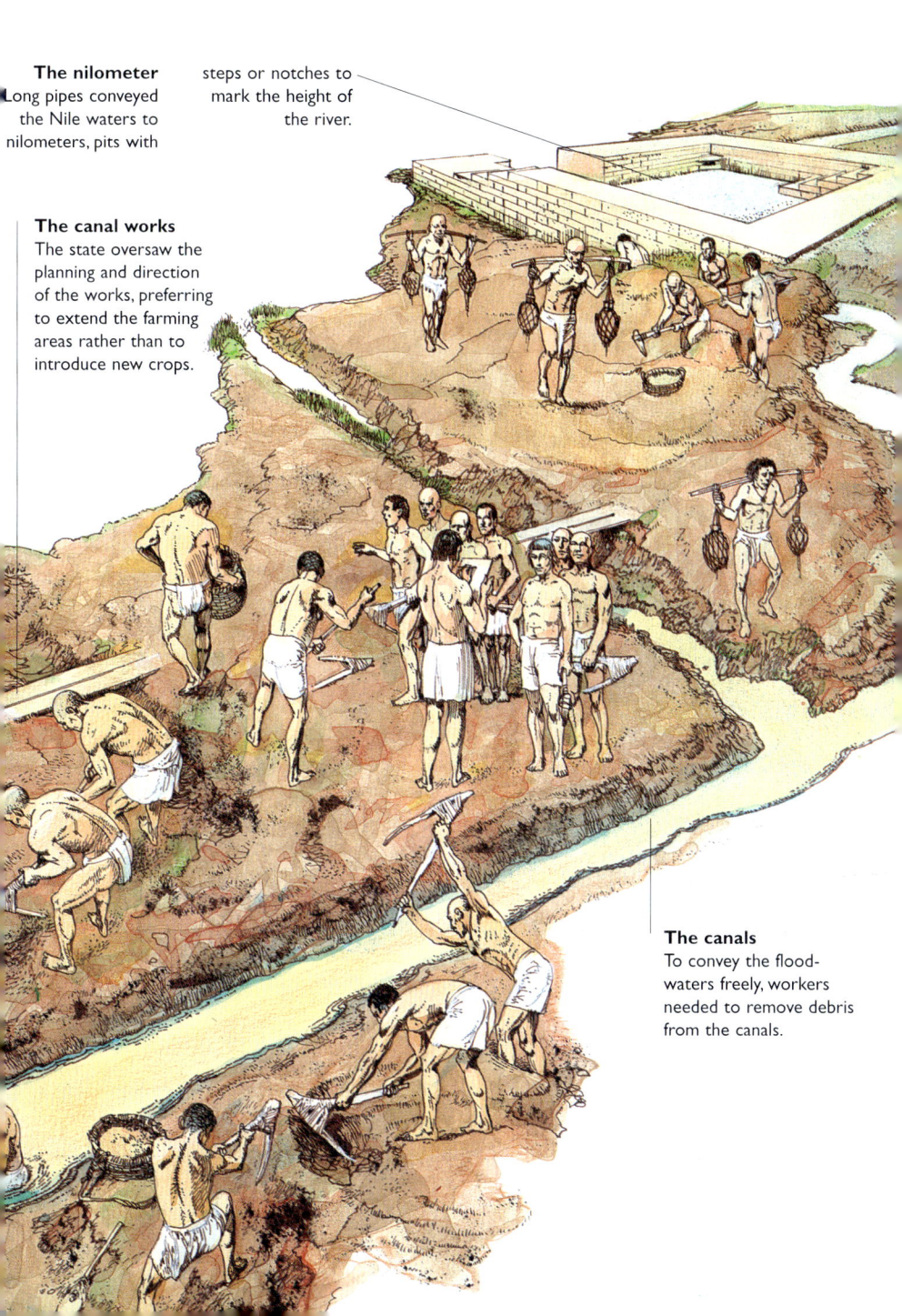

The nilometer Long pipes conveyed the Nile waters to nilometers, pits with steps or notches to mark the height of the river.

The canal works The state oversaw the planning and direction of the works, preferring to extend the farming areas rather than to introduce new crops.

The canals To convey the floodwaters freely, workers needed to remove debris from the canals.

The three seasons

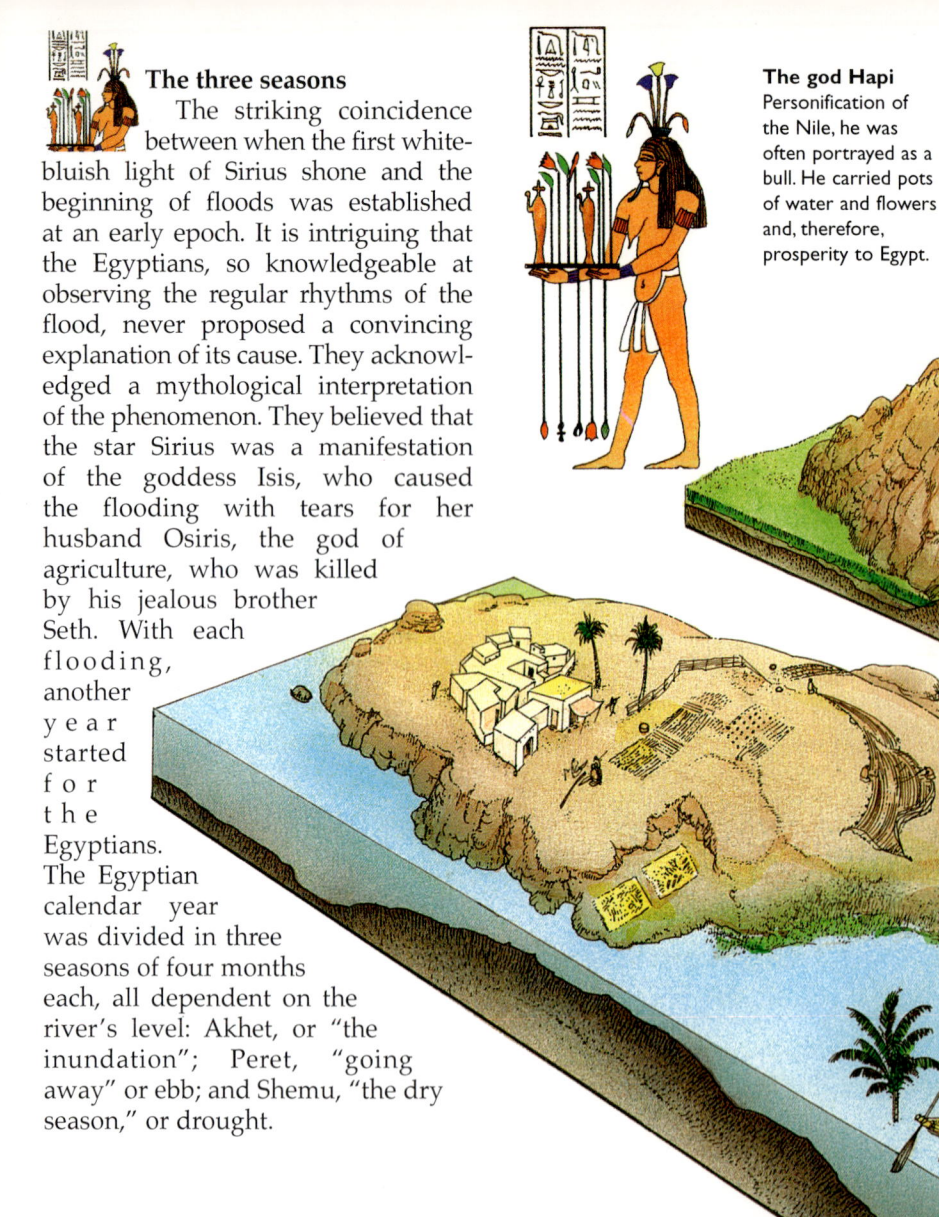

The striking coincidence between when the first white-bluish light of Sirius shone and the beginning of floods was established at an early epoch. It is intriguing that the Egyptians, so knowledgeable at observing the regular rhythms of the flood, never proposed a convincing explanation of its cause. They acknowledged a mythological interpretation of the phenomenon. They believed that the star Sirius was a manifestation of the goddess Isis, who caused the flooding with tears for her husband Osiris, the god of agriculture, who was killed by his jealous brother Seth. With each flooding, another year started for the Egyptians. The Egyptian calendar year was divided in three seasons of four months each, all dependent on the river's level: Akhet, or "the inundation"; Peret, "going away" or ebb; and Shemu, "the dry season," or drought.

The god Hapi
Personification of the Nile, he was often portrayed as a bull. He carried pots of water and flowers and, therefore, prosperity to Egypt.

Akhet
The period of flooding from July 19 to mid-November.

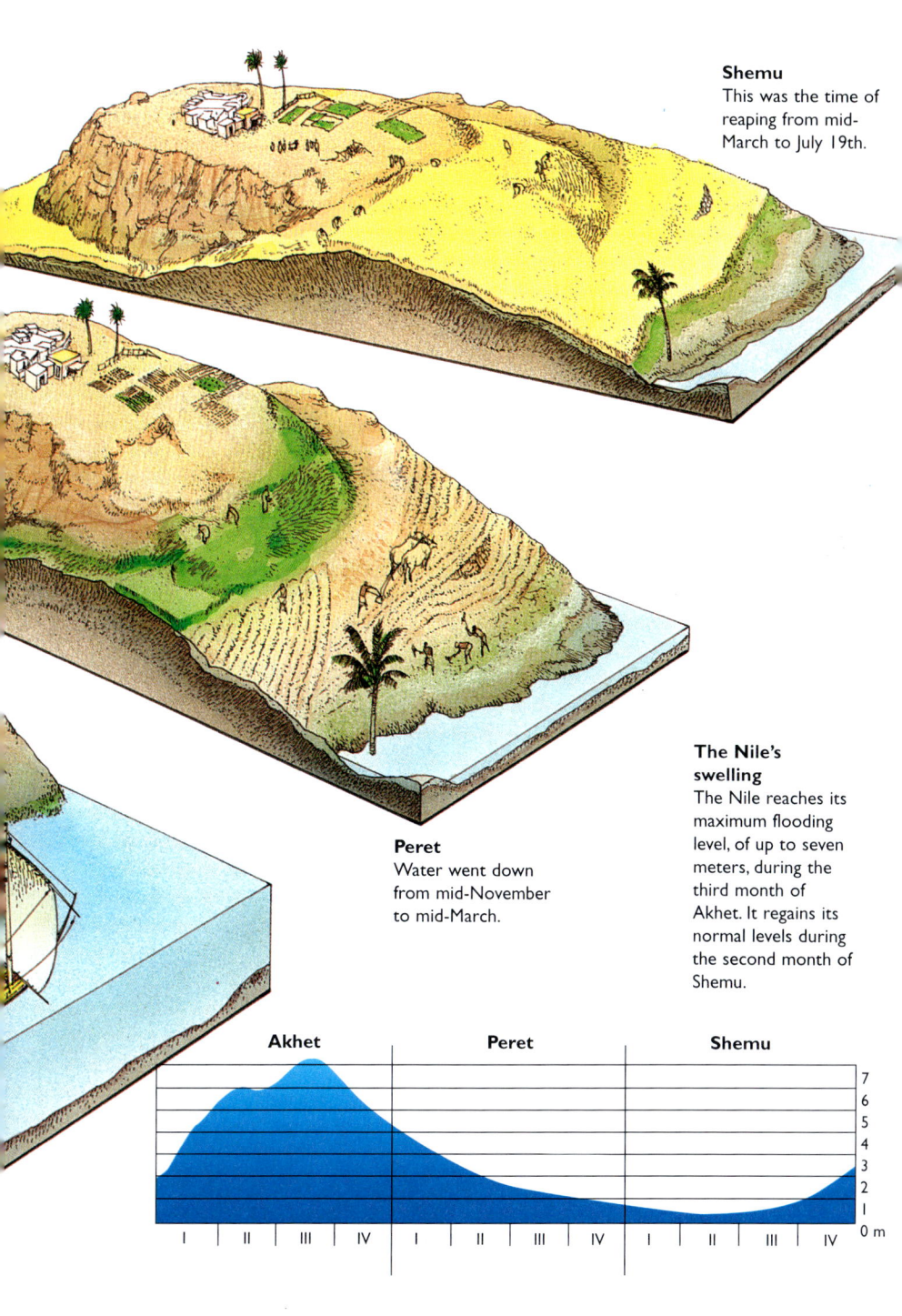

Shemu
This was the time of reaping from mid-March to July 19th.

Peret
Water went down from mid-November to mid-March.

The Nile's swelling
The Nile reaches its maximum flooding level, of up to seven meters, during the third month of Akhet. It regains its normal levels during the second month of Shemu.

Akhet	Peret	Shemu
I II III IV	I II III IV	I II III IV

Life in the fields: Akhet

Akhet lasted from July 19 to late autumn. During the flood, the peasants put their fieldwork aside, but were hardly idle. There were canals and ditches to free from debris, catch basins to reinforce and, eventually, to enlarge, and dams to repair or replace. Every peasant had to perform these tasks in obedience to state requirements. When water completely covered the tillable fields, farmers brought the livestock to higher, safer regions. Many Egyptians became fishermen and hunters. In fact, the flooding created areas of stagnant water, rich in organic

Reed Rafts
Useful and light, they were used for spear fishing and hunting as well as for big game like the hippopotamus.

Hunting in reed thickets
Hunters use traps, bird nets, bows, and throwing sticks, a type of heavy wooden boomerang.

Trawling nets and wickerwork fish traps
A team of fishermen pulls the net by hand as the rafts drag it in the shallow waters. Wickerwork fish traps do not require a collective effort, but they only catch few fish at a time.

At the village
Women prepare the food for storage: salted game and dried fish.

Work for everybody
Fixing nets, fishing spears, and hooks was work reserved for the elderly and weak.

FISHING AND HUNTING ALONG THE NILE
There were so many fish and hippopotami in the river, mongoose, and migratory birds in the reed thickets, that people seemed to be fishing and hunting in a big hatchery.

material, where fish abounded and many marsh birds nested along the banks.

Peret

When, around mid-November, the Nile waters gradually started to recede, the season of Peret began, which included the coldest months of the year. Plowing and sowing had to start without delay, because the silt left on the ground by the river dried quickly under the hot sun, creating a tough, caked crust that often had to be broken up with hoes or sticks. In the fields near the Nile, there was no need for hard preparatory work. Instead, farmers drove herds of animals over them so

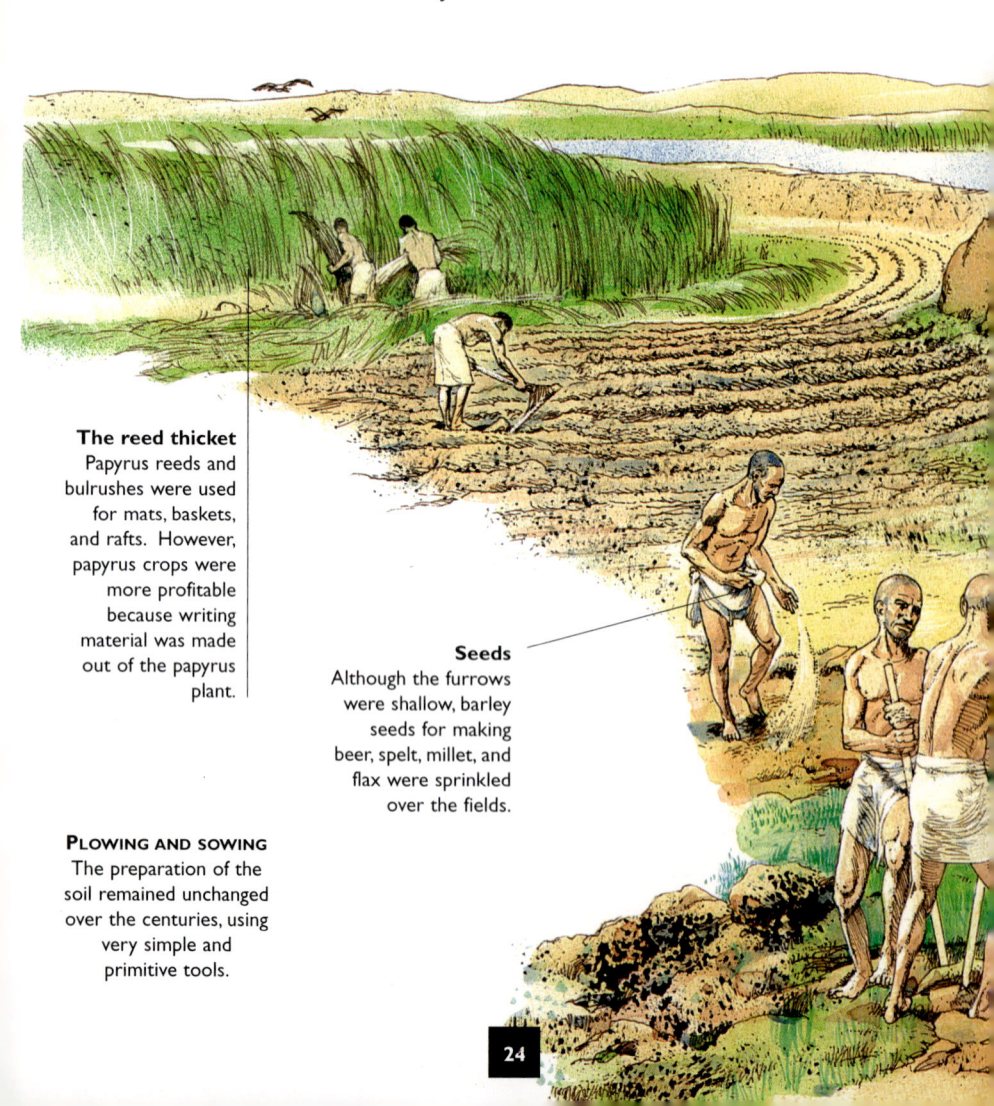

The reed thicket
Papyrus reeds and bulrushes were used for mats, baskets, and rafts. However, papyrus crops were more profitable because writing material was made out of the papyrus plant.

Seeds
Although the furrows were shallow, barley seeds for making beer, spelt, millet, and flax were sprinkled over the fields.

PLOWING AND SOWING
The preparation of the soil remained unchanged over the centuries, using very simple and primitive tools.

The vegetable garden
Various types of vegetables grew here, such as garlic, onions, and especially lettuce.

The plow
Pulled by two oxen, it was formed by a stake to which a rudimentary wooden ploughshare was bound. Relying on their muscles, peasants trod the plow in the flood-softened soil.

The hoe
It was made of wood and was used to crumble clods that the drying silt had hardened.

that they could plough the clods with their hooves and tread the seeds well into the soil.

This season demanded the continual irrigation of tillable fields. Special care was given to vegetable gardens. Moreover, ripe dates had to be picked from palms, and papyri and marsh reeds no longer covered in water had to be cut.

Shemu

The workload was heavier and more rushed at the onset of the last season: Shemu. It was time to harvest the fruits of the long days before the next flooding. In March, flax stems had to be cut,

THE HARVEST
It started in the regions of Upper and Middle Egypt where crops ripened earlier and moved to the Delta. The activity was punctuated by festivals and popular feasts, lasting several weeks.

The cattle
After the harvest, farm animals (oxen, but also ducks and geese) were driven to graze in the fields.

Gleaning
Women had to collect all the grain fallen on the ground so that nothing was wasted.

On the threshing floor
After the oxen and donkeys crushed the kernels to detach the grains, they were tossed in the air with short wooden paddles to remove the chaff.

Reaping
The grain was cut at knee-level by the reapers with wooden sickles with flint blades. Gathered in sheaves, it was carried on shoulders and placed into big baskets on the threshing floor.

The crew
An average cargo boat usually had ten oarsmen, two pilots, and one commander. It was very fast, serving as messenger and courier, and transported valuable, less bulky merchandise.

FLUVIAL TRAFFIC
There were harbors and strategic stations all along the course of the river. The responsibility of keeping the structures safe and running belonged to the closest villages.

and, at the beginning of summer, grapes and grain, which matured almost simultaneously in Upper Egypt and the central region of the Nile Valley, had to be reaped. Peasant bands, women and children included, moved from one field to another to harvest and tread grapes, to reap the grain, thresh it, and store it in huge silos under the watchful eyes of officials and scribes.

Sailing along the Nile

The Nile was also a great artery of communication, the only one in a region developed all along its length, surrounded by desert plateaus. Even during the dry season of Shemu, the

Arrivals and departures
Every day, a few boats traveled up and down a section of the river, like today's ferryboats do.

river was easily navigable, although sailors had to watch for dangerous extended sandbars. To descend towards the Delta, they relied on the current, which was quick or slow depending on the period. To boost the speed, oars and paddles were used. When sailors wanted to sail upstream, they hoisted sails, filled by the steady and regular winds coming from the Mediterranean Sea. Along the Nile, the main highway of Egypt, intensive trading developed, mostly in the Delta that connected the valley with the harbors on the Mediterranean.

THE OLD KINGDOM:
THE STATE

The 500 years of the Old Kingdom mark the golden age of ancient Egypt. Social and political institutions assumed the official form they kept for more than twenty centuries.

With the advent of the Third Dynasty, the Early Dynastic period ended, and the Old Kingdom began (2700–2200 B.C.). It proved to be the most creative period of Egyptian civilization, which lasted throughout the Sixth Dynasty.

At the beginning of this era, guiding principles were already upheld by the doctrine of harmony by Ma'at that freed the world from chaos and made it a good place to live. The state was presided over by a ministerial government, with a vizier (a non-Egyptian word): the same ministries for both of the kingdoms ruled over the primitive

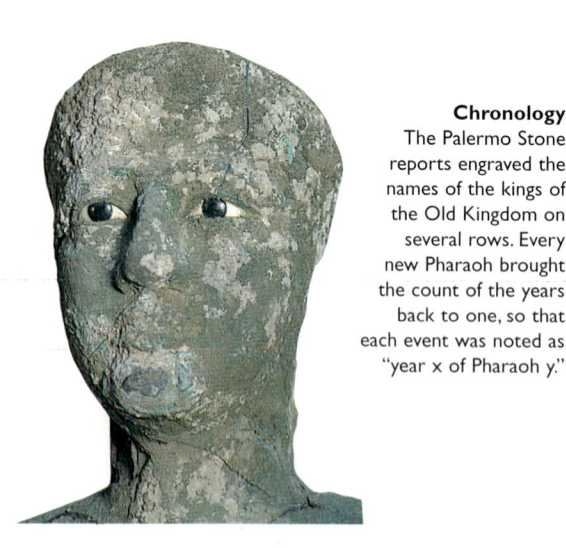

Chronology
The Palermo Stone reports engraved the names of the kings of the Old Kingdom on several rows. Every new Pharaoh brought the count of the years back to one, so that each event was noted as "year x of Pharaoh y."

The Pharaoh Pepi I
Pepi I of the 4th Dynasty began the construction of a canal on the Cataract of Aswan so that the Egyptian fleet directed to Nubia could easily pass it.

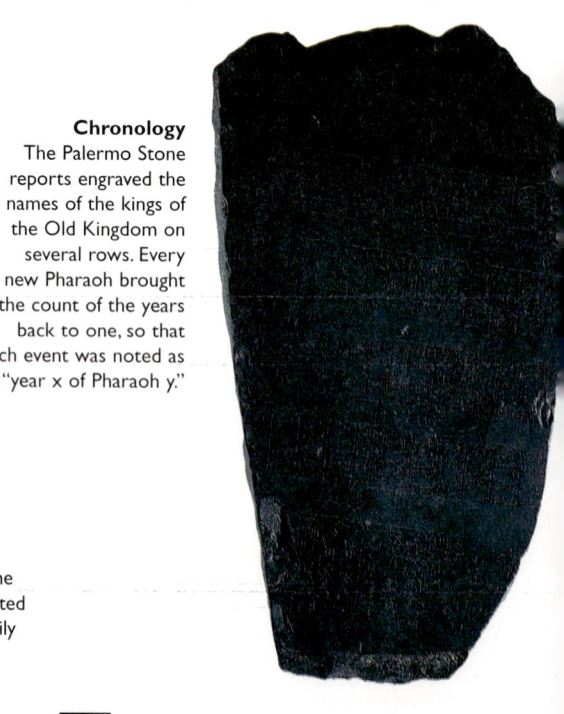

settlements, now transformed into provinces by governors' orders. At the same time, officials conducted a census and took periodic measurements of the Nile's height. The alphabetic writing system, more suitable for keeping records, was adopted together with decimal numbering. Mastery of arts and crafts surged to a high level, and language, arts, and sciences developed, especially medicine. Above all, however, what became more important was the idea of the divine in terms of eternity, infinity, omnipotence, and omniscience.

Memphis: a chosen city

During the Early Pre-dynastic period, sovereigns had ruled from Thinis, in Upper Egypt, but after the Third Dynasty, Memphis, in the north, became the capital. Memphis, a walled city nestled around an archaic white palace, was an important religious center, but not the foremost. In the same region, Heliopolis was a rival and Saqqara and Giza were the sites chosen for both royal and private burials.

Politically stable and immune from external attacks, Egypt needed only to defend its external borders. Libyan attempts to invade the Delta had been repeatedly defeated, and the Egyptians kept the Sinai Peninsula constantly under surveillance to protect precious stones and copper—used, together with tin, for bronze weapons—that were mined there. A mild protectorate was employed over Byblos in Phoenicia, sources of timber, unavailable in Egypt. In the south, instead, the Pharaoh Snefru, first king of the Fourth Dynasty, organized expeditions in

A special corp
Since the first expeditions to Nubia, armies of archers were trained to guarantee public order and the personal safety of the pharaoh.

Nubia to acquire the granite for the pyramids.

Sahure, forerunner of the Fifth Dynasty, sent naval expeditions to Levant and Punt, the legendary regions of the Red Sea, and to the Horn of Africa, bountiful source of spices, ivory, gold, and incense.

However, the kings of the Fifth and Sixth Dynasties (2510–2200 B.C.) did not seem sure of their power and demanded the support of the governors sent to administer the several provinces, especially the southern ones, which were far from the capital. To gain their loyalty, the kings gave them more powers

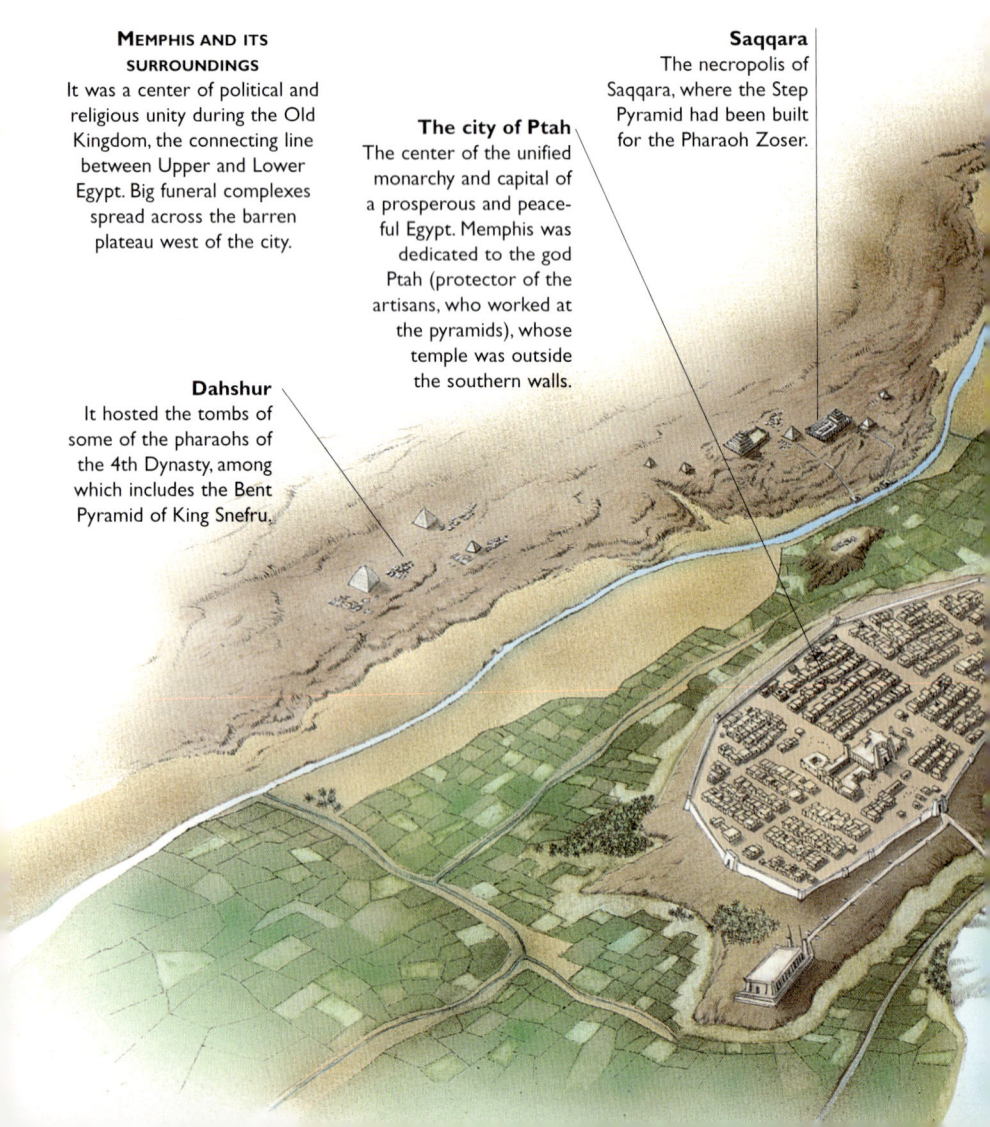

MEMPHIS AND ITS SURROUNDINGS
It was a center of political and religious unity during the Old Kingdom, the connecting line between Upper and Lower Egypt. Big funeral complexes spread across the barren plateau west of the city.

The city of Ptah
The center of the unified monarchy and capital of a prosperous and peaceful Egypt. Memphis was dedicated to the god Ptah (protector of the artisans, who worked at the pyramids), whose temple was outside the southern walls.

Saqqara
The necropolis of Saqqara, where the Step Pyramid had been built for the Pharaoh Zoser.

Dahshur
It hosted the tombs of some of the pharaohs of the 4th Dynasty, among which includes the Bent Pyramid of King Snefru.

and vast lands to exploit and so increased their independence from central authority. The granting of privileges soon followed, particularly during the long reign of Pepi II of the Sixth Dynasty. The most dangerous privilege of all was permission to transmit their titles to their heirs.

The Civil Administration

The Egyptian state has always remained centralized, with a pyramidal organizational structure established during the Old Kingdom.

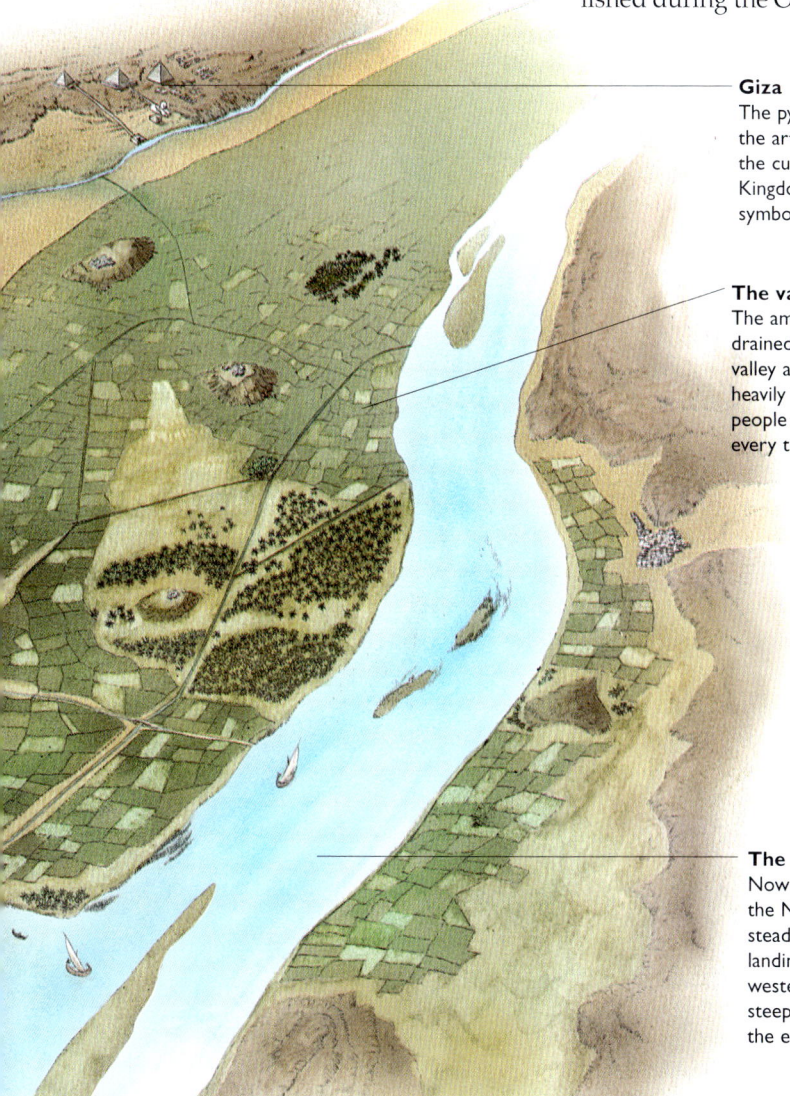

Giza
The pyramids of Giza: the artistic hallmark of the culture of the Old Kingdom and an eternal symbol of Egypt.

The valley
The ample and well-drained fields make the valley around Memphis heavily populated with people and adapted to every type of crop.

The river
Now close to its Delta, the Nile flows slowly and steadily. It has several landings on the shallow western coast and is also steep here and there on the eastern coast.

The king or pharaoh had absolute power over a population estimated between two and five million inhabitants. He established government conduct and promoted state projects. Most of the executive power, however, was delegated to the vizier. He headed a highly efficient administration, and was also portrayed in Narmer's palette. The vizier acted in cooperation with the chiefs of the main sectors, in the top ranks of the civil servants. They acted as emissaries of the king, who was the living source of the law, passing on the sovereign's orders to second-rank officials in charge of local justice, economy, finance, agriculture, and important civil projects.

The ancient Egyptians felt incredibly strongly about hierarchy and work. Officials of any order and rank responded with loyalty and promptness to their superiors and acted towards their subordinates with full respect of the law.

Officials in higher ranks—the ministers, as we would say today—were the *mer*, "those in whom the mouth is" (those able to command), controlled by the king or vizier's inspectors. Every ministry had several servants of lesser rank, such as secretaries, scribes, and filing clerks. Governors, directly nominated by the pharaoh, locally chosen and fired at will, man-

The vizier
The vizier Rekhmire, in a tomb painting, with the crook, symbol of leadership, on his right hand and the scepter in his left.

The social pyramid
Egyptian society had a pyramidal structure. At the top reigned the pharaoh, who delegated his power to a class of court officials. They obeyed his orders like the rest of the population to whom they passed them on.

THE POWER STRUCTURE

It remained unchanged throughout the pharaonic age, although, during the New Kingdom, the vizier took on more responsibilities as the head of the entire bureaucracy.

The Great House
There is an official at its head. It includes the pharaoh's family members, the court, and the sovereign's personal assistants.

Vizier

Pharaoh

The House of the King
The royal chancellery, the depository of royal decrees, and the registry of deeds.

The White House
Controls the flow of wheat, gold, and precious materials into the central warehouses.

The House of Gold
Redistributes the riches of the Great House in the form of consumer goods to the Great House itself, the officials, the state workers, and the temples.

State property
Investigates the condition of all public possessions.

Public works
Finances and projects the construction of temples, palaces, and pyramids.

Canals
Presides over the construction and maintenance of all the canals.

The cult
Under the orders of an official, it oversees the temples of the pyramids, the solar temples, and the sanctuaries of Heliopolis.

Civil affairs
Checks the work of the governors of the provinces and has a civil police.

The judiciary
Administered by the High Court (the Charter of the Six) and controls the local courts.

Military forces
Mostly, it deals with the corvée of the workers recruited for the huge construction sites.

aged the districts (*nomoi*), areas similar to the present-day provinces. Working with them was a state official, who, in the provinces, performed the same duties accomplished in the capital by the vizier. Upper Egypt had twenty-two provinces; in Lower Egypt the number grew from thirteen to seventeen.

Governors with special police duties governed the Western Oases, which were subject to Libyan raids. They were chosen from among the enlisted military personnel, who had meager opportunities to acquire more prestige. During this period, Egypt, protected by deserts and sea, had little need to fight enemies.

Already in the Old Kingdom, social class distribution was fluid: the population seems to have been distributed in a hierarchy with many steps. At the top, there were gods (and the pharaoh), with the vizier underneath, then the court offi-

Menkaure
Relief in green schist of Menkaure pictures a pharaoh of the 4th Dynasty (2532–2504 B.C.), who wears the white crown of Upper Egypt and a false beard, symbol of his divine power. The goddess Hathor (on his right) and a local divinity accompany him.

Khafre
Detail of the statue, in diorite, of Khafre, pharaoh of the 4th Dynasty (2558–2532 B.C.). The god Horus, as a falcon, stretches its wing over the *nemes*, the royal head cloth.

cials and their assistants, until the last servant. On such a scale, except for the first and the last steps, everyone else was both in charge and under charge, a situation that allowed one to either become well integrated into the community or, for the smartest, to improve their positions.

The pharaoh and the Egyptian society

The pharaoh symbolized and supported the state. He embodied Ma'at and guaranteed bliss and organization to the country. He was the intermediary between the human and the divine worlds, the eternal guarentor of the order and harmony of the universe, which otherwise would have sunk into chaos. Of the five names that were attributed to the pharaoh, the first ones referred to his divine origin: Horus, the falcon-god protector of the unification; the Two Ladies, with whom he identified himself, Nekhbet and Uto, the goddesses of the South and North Kingdoms; and golden Horus. The fourth element, "Son of Re" (the sun god), which referred to his civil power and meant "king," followed by his birth name. With the magic force that emanated from him, the pharaoh ensured fertility to earth, prosperity for the population, and strength to the armies. His authority was absolute and unquestioned. Being Ma'at's spiritual son, he pro-

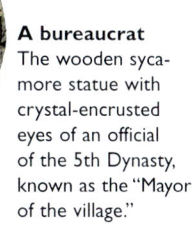

A bureaucrat
The wooden sycamore statue with crystal-encrusted eyes of an official of the 5th Dynasty, known as the "Mayor of the village."

claimed just and balanced decrees, which had the effect of inspired decisions. It was the duty of the vizier, his right hand man, to ensure their total compliance, as human errors could not alter divine justice.

The vizier, therefore, was in charge of both the bureaucratic apparatus and was the chief executive administrator of justice. He was the official who designated the courts and monitored their conduct because truth was the pharaoh's prerogative and all his servants, men or women, rich or poor, were equal before the law. The god-king even delegated his religious authority. He transferred it to priests, who represented him during the celebration of ceremonies. Egypt honored a great number of gods, and the many sacred ceremonies required, over time, an increasing number of temple servants.

At the beginning of the Old Kingdom, the governors of the provinces were also the high priests of the local temples and the recipients of the income derived from the goods offered to the temple. However, at the end of the Old Kingdom, when lands and immunity were conferred on governors, the temples they administered became both rich and autonomous. Different duties were assigned to secondary priests (administrators, chiefs of production), which confirmed the rigorous hierarchies.

Wealth distribution

Egypt and its riches belonged to the pharaoh, who had to provide subsis-

Near the top
An Egyptian couple, in painted limestone, of Prince Rahotep and the Princess Nefret, a high official of the royal family and his wife.

Pharaoh and priest
A pharaoh (recognizable by the blue crown, worn only in war times and during solemn ceremonies) dressed as a priest: a leopard skin is thrown over his shoulders.

tence, security, and possibly well-being to his people, according to Ma'at, which asked for reciprocity, solidarity, and responsibility in all areas of life. The economy was regulated by a distribution system whose center was the temple. In every region, produce or goods were brought to the main temple. Here, scribe-priests catalogued and stored them before redistributing them among the population. In exchange for the priests' equitable and careful distribution of food and products, temples were generously made tax-exempt. Private property existed as small farming companies and artisan family-owned shops, whose goods (livestock, tools, and fishing boats) were counted and taxed annually. People did business by bartering. Everything had its own value.

No slaves in Egypt

The concepts of order, harmony, reciprocity, and solidarity in business conformed to Ma'at. The higher classes had the privilege of wealth, but remained subject, like all servants, to the power that only the pharaoh possessed. For the same reason, slavery, in the sense of a total absence of legal rights, did not exist in the Old Kingdom.

Sometimes, a few workers could have been rented out by the landowners or the temples that employed them. These were very poor people, reduced to a state of servility that was neither defini-

Enemies at their feet
Two war prisoners (an Asian and a Syrian) painted on the soles of a pair of sandals, despised, but not slaves.

Free men
For a long time, scholars believed that the workers who built the pyramids and temples (opposite) were slaves. Instead, they were free men with a regular contract.

tive nor hereditary. They were not considered objects or soulless machines. Most of those reduced to this state were farmers, but artisans and scribes also worked in this way.

The scribes' lifestyle

Besides the court officials who shared the pharaoh's power, insofar as an absolute and divine power could be shared, there were the lower bureaucratic ranks. No other ancient civilization enjoyed such a comprehensive administration. The scribes, numerous and respected, shared a highly specialized profession but were otherwise not

No captives
Even when, during the New Kingdom, the Egyptians went to war, their captives were soon integrated in the economic life of the country. From the tomb of Thutmose IV, pharaoh of the 18th Dynasty: *Submission of a prisoner*.

a homogeneous group. They had gone to school for many years to learn the complex Egyptian writing system. The least fortunate among them spent their lives writing dictation for higher officers. Others, though, were given more responsibilities and intervened in all the aspects of community life.

They worked in administrative offices, in the fields to measure, to count the cattle, or to estimate the crop yields; at the borders to check traffic and monitor foreigners; in short, anywhere there was a need to collect taxes.

The survival of the population depended on their precision and skill. In fact, their task was not simply to count and estimate the wealth amassed, but to forecast lean years, when the floods were too violent or too weak, resulting in famine. When this occurred, they had to alert the people and provide for emergency supplies.

The scribe was a proud worker regardless of his role and function.

In *The Satire of the Trades*, an ancient text says, "The washer washes every day—and vigorously too—the laundry of the neighbors . . . The potter's hands and feet are covered with clay . . . The shoemaker mixes the tanning and its smell is awful . . . But the scribe oversees the work of them all. Take note!"

Writing

In a way, it was true that the scribes' job, compared to those of craftsmen and farmers, was generally not as physically demanding, it consisted primarily of writing, a difficult but certainly not exhausting task.

Scribe at work
Updated by the chief civil engineer, the scribe records the daily progress of work in the construction site of a pharaoh, calculating the costs of the materials and of the provisions, the workers' wages, unexpected expenses, and even accidents.

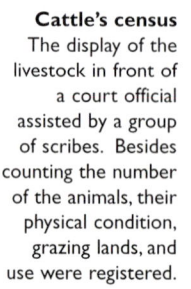

Cattle's census
The display of the livestock in front of a court official assisted by a group of scribes. Besides counting the number of the animals, their physical condition, grazing lands, and use were registered.

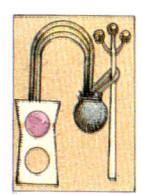

How to advertise for a scribe
A hieroglyph formed by scribe's tools: a palette with two wells, for the black and red ink pigments, a water pot, and a reed pen.

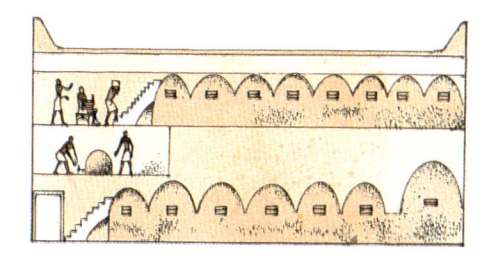

The scribe's kit
The scribe's writing equipment: various types of quill pens (brushes), a spatula to dilute the pigments, and ink. Papyrus rolls, filed in sealed vases, made up the library and the filing system of the temple.

Accountants
Scribes punctually recorded every administrative act: the daily wages of a worker, a sack of grain stored in warehouses, or a list of offerings to a deity.

File clerks
Many scribes copied scientific and literary texts, ritual and magic formulae. Papyrus rolls, filed in sealed vases, made up the library and the filing system of the temple.

Egyptian writing was made from pictures (hieroglyphs), representing either people or the world around them. Very early in its development, each hieroglyphic sign was used as a pictogram; that is, it conveyed its meaning with a symbol that resembled an object. Later, the need to communicate abstract concepts and proper names introduced the use of phonetic signs along the principle of "rebus." As trades developed, a quicker system of signs was needed. Therefore, hieroglyphs started to be drawn in a stylized manner. The Greeks called this writing hieratic (priestly), because to the best of their knowledge it was used only by priests to transcribe sacred texts. Originally, however, it was generally used. In later ages (seventh century B.C.) an even faster and simpler writing was developed, suitable for daily necessities. It was derived from hieratic writing and was called demotic, that is, popular.

The artisans

Manual work had always been considered one of the fundamental values of society. The artisan was viewed as an artist. For example, Imhotep, vizier and architect of the Pharaoh Zoser, for whom he built the Step Pyramid of Saqqara, started his career as a stone pot maker. Those who were not farmers were artisans. Although craftsmanship was booming (jewelry, decorated earthenware, and furnishings), it satisfied only internal demand. Large external trade was a state monopoly, managed exclusively by the pharaoh. Craftsmen rarely worked autonomous-

Reading the hieroglyphs
Usually, hieroglyphs are read from top to bottom and from right to left. The direction is indicated by the heads of the figures of people or animals which are turned to the side where the inscription begins.

Harvesting the papyri
Reapers cut papyrus reeds in a marsh. Plaster from the tomb of the landowner Ti at Saqqara (c. 2500 B.C.).

Instead of paper
Papyrus stems, cut lengthwise into thin strips, arranged crosswise in two layers and dried with a glue, supplied the writing material.

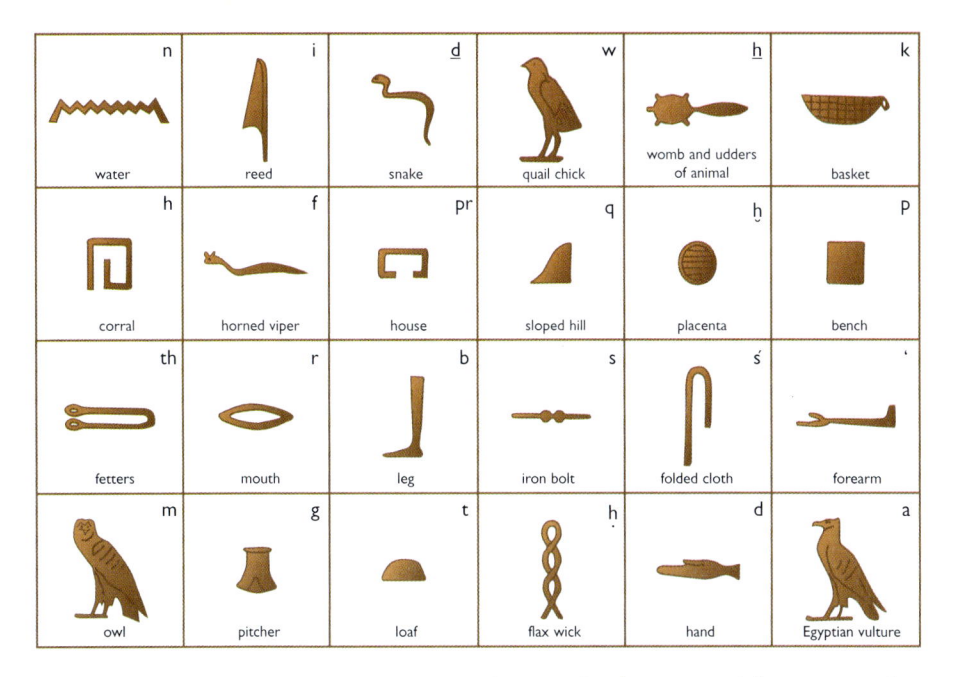

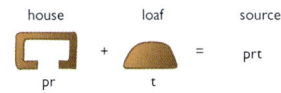

n — water	i — reed	d — snake	w — quail chick	ḥ — womb and udders of animal	k — basket
h — corral	f — horned viper	pr — house	q — sloped hill	ḫ — placenta	p — bench
th — fetters	r — mouth	b — leg	s — iron bolt	ś — folded cloth	' — forearm
m — owl	g — pitcher	t — loaf	ḥ — flax wick	d — hand	a — Egyptian vulture

Like a rebus
Table of hieroglyphs and of the sound of single letters. The combination of more signs (and sounds) created different words and meanings.

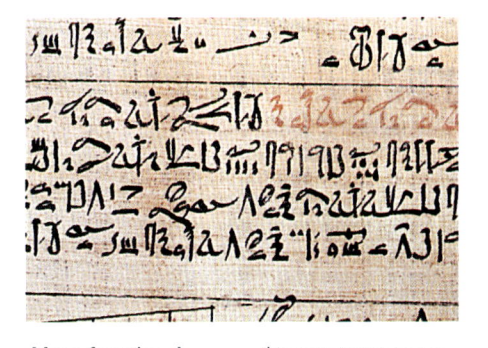

house + loaf = source
pr + t = prt

More functional
A geometry problem in hieratic. Obviously, in this case, it was impossible to use hieroglyphs.

ly. Usually they served the state or the temple from which they received payments in goods (foods, clothing, sandals, and salt) as well as other basic services (housing, working tools and equipment, medical assistance, and burial). Craftsmen passed their trade secrets from father to son and were accustomed to hiring apprentices. In *The Satire of the Trades*, young Egyptians were free to choose a profession according to their natural inclinations, but they were cautioned against possible difficulties, to encourage them instead to enter an administrative career or the school of scribes. Until the Fourth Dynasty, craftsmen were commonly employed in building pyramids and later, during the Fifth Dynasty, temple sites. They were quarrymen, stonemasons, carpenters, woodworkers, smelters, sculptors, plasterers, and painters. They learned to handle all stones, as well as any type of wood and metal (not yet of iron). With the advent of the Sixth Dynasty, however, the building frenzy that had animated fifty generations of craftsmen for more than two-and-a-half centuries almost came to a halt. Gathering in the capital, without the support of a social system that guaranteed them jobs and food, they organized a social revolt in 2260 B.C., the first one ever recorded. This uprising weakened the pharaoh's power and contributed to anarchy, which in turn led to the First Intermediate period.

The farmers

If the country was in good econom-

Making beer
One of the most important daily tasks usually performed by women. From Saqqara, a small limestone statue from the 5th Dynasty.

Wooden art
Wooden painted beauty case with a spoon to mix ointments.

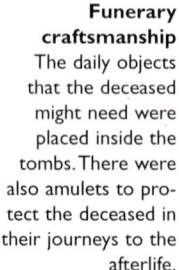

Funerary craftsmanship
The daily objects that the deceased might need were placed inside the tombs. There were also amulets to protect the deceased in their journeys to the afterlife.

ic shape, it was because of farmers, who worked either independently or for a powerful landowner (an official or the temple). In this case, farmers were leased or rented their labor, but remained free. The majority of peasants lived in villages, swarming with parasites, next to the farm lands. They paid a tribute in goods calculated by the scribes based on extension, productivity, cattle or draft animals, fruit trees, or reed thickets. They had to provide the country with wheat for bread, barley for beer, meat for the table, linen for garments, and papyrus for boats and writing material. They had at their disposal simple but useful tools, like the mattock, a short wooden hoe to break the soil, and a light plough. The flood of the Nile, however, because of the fer-

Goldsmith's work
This sacred falcon with obsidian eyes and a plumed golden crown with the cobra goddess (the sacred-royal cobra) shows the high level of craftsmanship in the 4th Dynasty.

tilizing silt it left behind, relieved them from the drudgery of year-round farming, as it was not necessary to plough deeply. During the months of flooding, peasants were obliged to work on state projects. Whatever their condition was, they enjoyed protection from external dangers, foods of above-average quality, the possibility of participating in sacred rituals, and the hope that their children would live in better conditions.

INSPECTION
State officials come to the village for the annual budget, the census of the inhabitants, and the inventory of stocks.

Taxes
The chief inspector calculates the percentage of the products owed to the pharaoh and demands it.

Enlisting
The youngest and strongest peasants are chosen to be sent to the large construction sites. They were obliged to leave their village and families.

Tax collectors mistreat tardy debtors
Not everybody could afford to pay the state taxes. Armed guards enforced the rules.

THE VILLAGE
Not far from the river or the canals, it was formed by a series of windowless dwellings made of unbaked, mud bricks. Light and air came through the door only.

THE OLD KINGDOM:
THE RELIGION

During the Old Kingdom, the religion of the Egyptians gave great importance to the funerary cult that is linked to absolute faith in life after death. Already during the early ages, many deities populated the Egyptian pantheon.

These two religious manifestations, the funerary and the divine, coexisted since Egypt's origins. Funerary religion was based on the belief in the soul's eternal survival and death was considered only the separation from the body of this spiritual force, the *ka*, the person's "double," which had found a material home in the body. As the world had been created by the vital force of the universe, the eternal spirit had to return to order and harmony, transcending humanity, as soon as its sojourn on earth ended. It is still the logic of the Ma'at applied to the sacred. As for the strictly divine aspect of Egyptian religion, the high number of deities is not surprising. In fact, all the chiefdoms' local divinities, often represented as animals or a combination of them, had also been welcomed. They were probably cult legacies of prehis-

Osiris
The god Osiris handling the crook and flail scepters, signs of his power. His green face and green hand symbolize the perennial cycle of plant life.

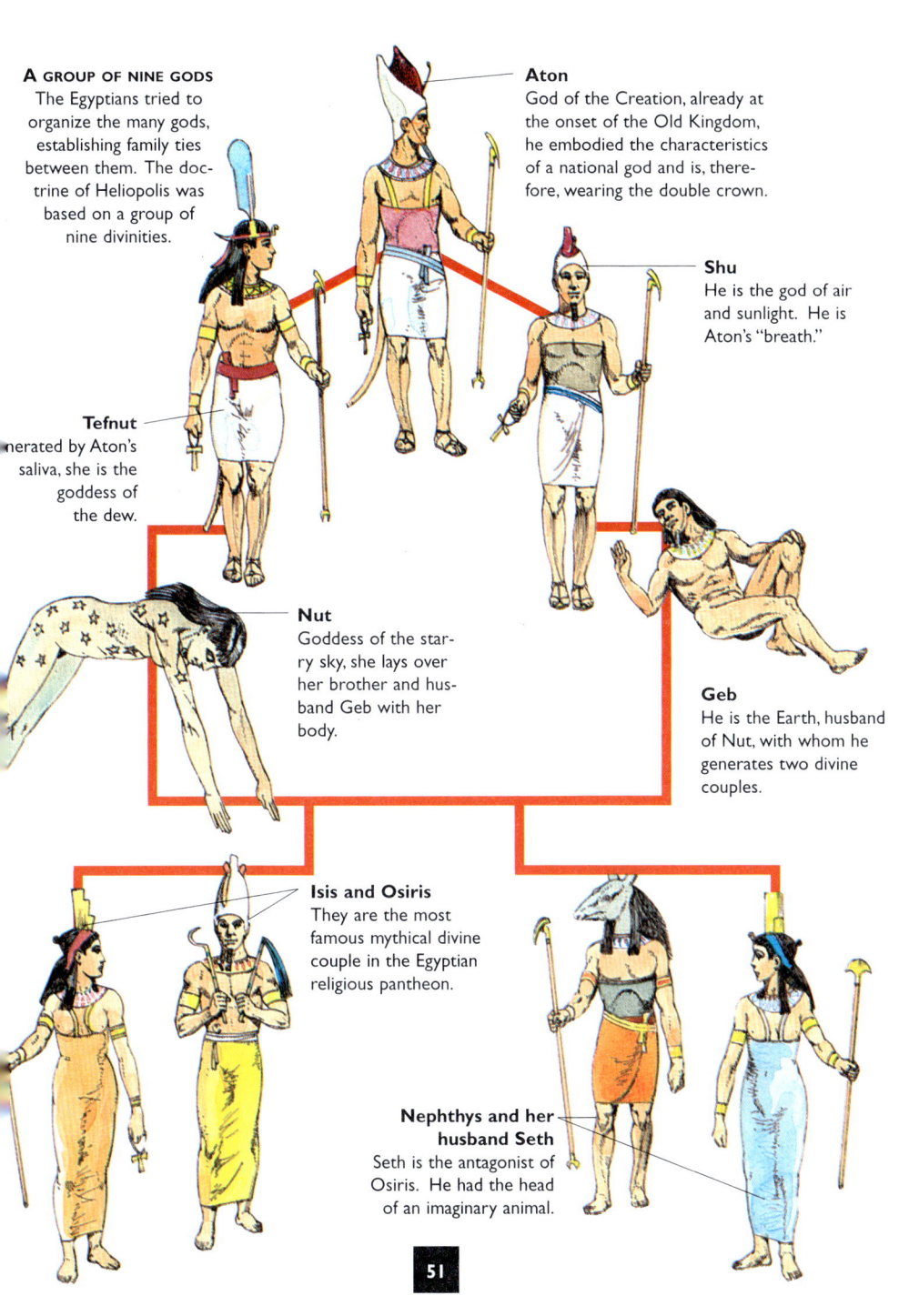

A GROUP OF NINE GODS
The Egyptians tried to organize the many gods, establishing family ties between them. The doctrine of Heliopolis was based on a group of nine divinities.

Aton
God of the Creation, already at the onset of the Old Kingdom, he embodied the characteristics of a national god and is, therefore, wearing the double crown.

Shu
He is the god of air and sunlight. He is Aton's "breath."

Tefnut
Generated by Aton's saliva, she is the goddess of the dew.

Nut
Goddess of the starry sky, she lays over her brother and husband Geb with her body.

Geb
He is the Earth, husband of Nut, with whom he generates two divine couples.

Isis and Osiris
They are the most famous mythical divine couple in the Egyptian religious pantheon.

Nephthys and her husband Seth
Seth is the antagonist of Osiris. He had the head of an imaginary animal.

toric tribes to their own totems. The Egyptians did not concern themselves with clear-cut attributes and powers for each single god, although they trusted some with a precise role. For them, gods were superior beings who, following their fancies, decided the course of the world and with whom they had to maintain good relations. This was the pharaoh's duty, as the living god, and the purpose of the religious ceremonies held in temples. However, in state liturgy, the sun god in all its manifestations prevailed: Khepri in the morning, Re at noon, and Aton in the evening. Its cult was spread by the priests of Heliopolis (which in Greek means "the City of the Sun"), north of Memphis. They elaborated the first theological doctrine (*Ennead*) based on a group of nine gods. Other towns, like Hermopolis and Memphis, built different theologies based on a group of eight gods (*Ogdoad*). Besides these cults, another developed, which sprung from an earlier age, dedicated to Osiris.

The Ennead of Heliopolis

Nobody created Aton, the sun god who set in motion the Creation from the primordial chaos. He created a divine couple, Shu, god of the air, and Tefnut, goddess of the dew. From their union, another couple was born: Geb, god of the earth, and Nut, goddess of the sky. Geb and Nut gave life to two other divine couples, Seth and Nephthys, and Isis and Osiris. This last couple was worshiped throughout the country until the end of the Egyptian civilization. In fact, it lasted even longer, because it also spread to the Greco-Roman world. According to the myth, Osiris was killed by his evil brother, Seth, and his dismembered body was

The sun god Re
Falcon-headed god, personifying the sun at midday. For this reason, he has a luminous sun disk over his head.

Isis
The goddess on her throne with Horus as a child.

Hathor

Amon

Horus

Khonsu

Nephthys

Khnum

Local deities
Before Egypt's unification, every settlement had its own god, so the unified country amassed a large assortment of gods. Different cults gave life to a complex and sometimes contradictory religion.

scattered throughout the world. Isis, however, went in tears looking for all the parts of her husband's body, used her magic arts to restore him to wholeness, and breathed life into them. Resurrected, Osiris became the god of the underworld.

The cult of the dead

Both the sacred story, which recounted Osiris's death and resurrection, and the daily recurrence of the sun god, who at sunset is engulfed by darkness to rise up again in triumph in the morning, convinced the Egyptians that the soul survives after death. For this to happen, the soul required that the body be neither decayed nor dissolved. This is why the dead body had to be preserved, using mummification, burial ceremonies, and tombs. In older ages, a true life in the afterlife was considered the pharaoh's exclusive privilege, and his subjects hoped just that his immortality would be extended to them. Later, at the end of the Old Kingdom, survival became the right of those who could afford a tomb and the cost of funeral rituals.

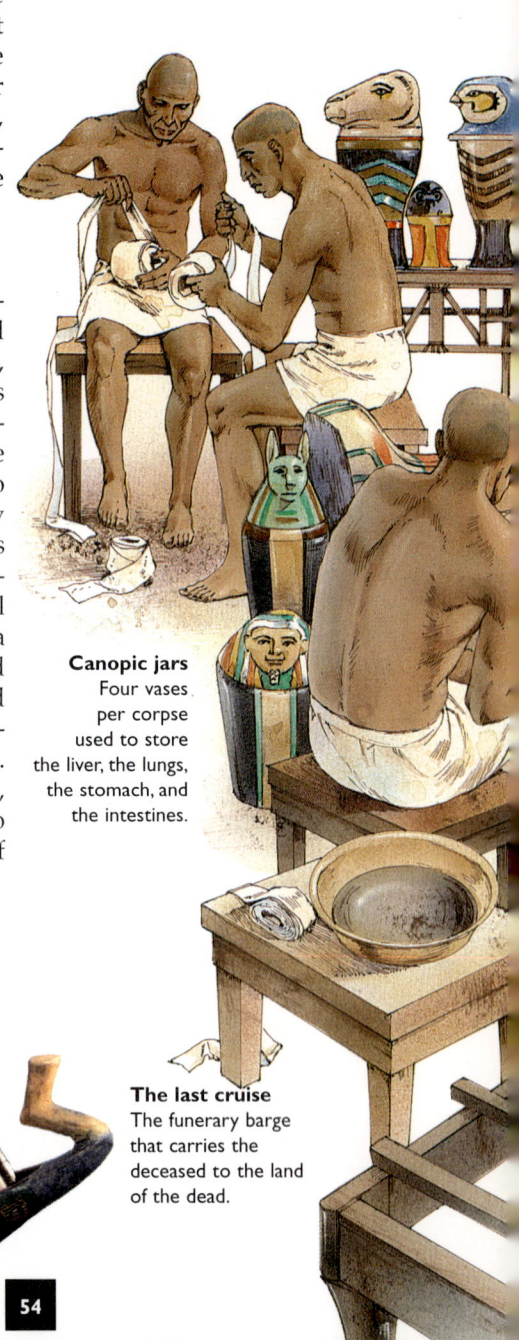

Canopic jars
Four vases per corpse used to store the liver, the lungs, the stomach, and the intestines.

The last cruise
The funerary barge that carries the deceased to the land of the dead.

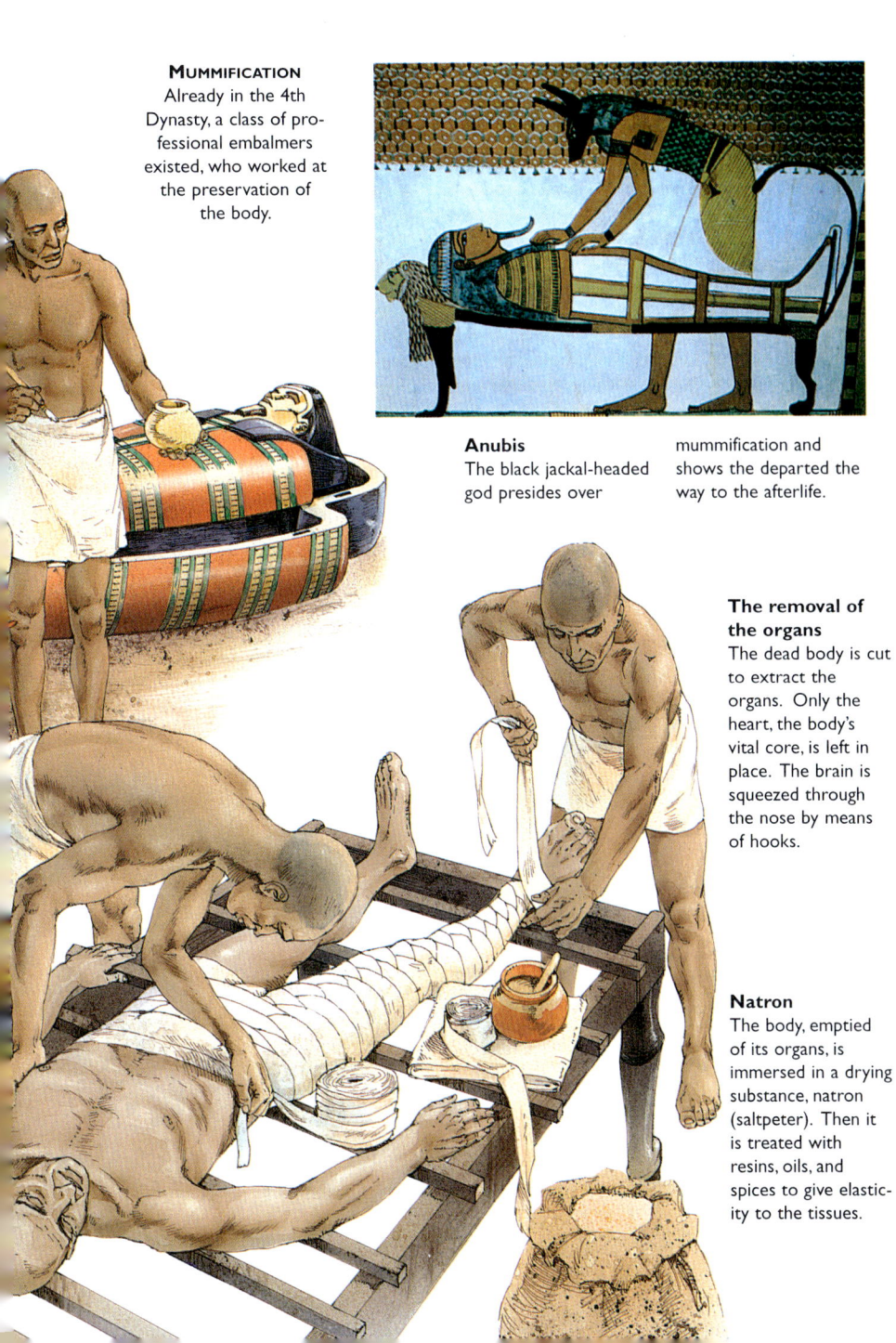

MUMMIFICATION
Already in the 4th Dynasty, a class of professional embalmers existed, who worked at the preservation of the body.

Anubis
The black jackal-headed god presides over mummification and shows the departed the way to the afterlife.

The removal of the organs
The dead body is cut to extract the organs. Only the heart, the body's vital core, is left in place. The brain is squeezed through the nose by means of hooks.

Natron
The body, emptied of its organs, is immersed in a drying substance, natron (saltpeter). Then it is treated with resins, oils, and spices to give elasticity to the tissues.

The pyramids

Since the Early Dynastic period, the royal tomb was strictly an outward manifestation of power on earth. With the Third Dynasty, it also became the symbol of the pharaoh's divinity, celestial survival, and rule, which defeated death. To express these new religious and philosophical ideas, Imhotep, vizier and architect of the Pharaoh Zoser (2670–2650 B.C.), designed a tomb called a mastaba. The Step Pyramid of Saqqara was built as a symbol of a stairway pointing to the sky to let the pharaoh climb to heaven. The idea of the pyramid was so successful that in the next forty years, between 2670 and

THE GIZA COMPLEX
A southern view of the pyramids of Giza. Their real dimensions cannot be perceived in this perspective.

A PROVERB
An Arab proverb pays homage to the pyramids of Giza, already more than 4,500 years old: "Time challenges everything, but the pyramids challenge time."

The pyramid of Menkaure
The smallest of the pyramids of Giza (it is only 216 ft. tall with a base of 346 x 346 ft.) has kept its original granite coating despite many removals over the centuries.

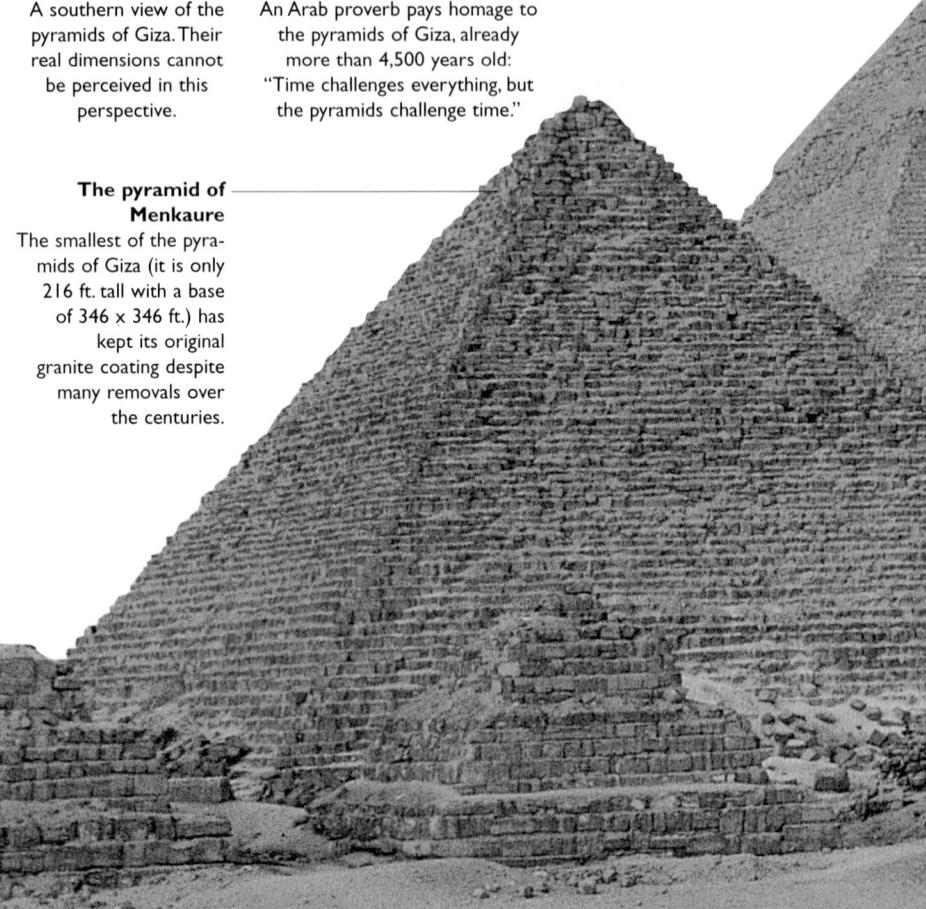

2630 B.C., another eleven pyramids were built. One hundred years later, under the kingdom of Snefru, the first pharaoh of the Fourth Dynasty, the pyramid acquired its distinctive form, with straight sides. This formal change is remarkable as it clearly shows how important the association between solar and royal cults had become. The connection should have risen spontaneously in the mind of the observer: the edges of the pyramids of Giza copied the angles of the sunrays, and its sloping sides were stone representations of the rays sent to earth from heaven. The whitish external coating was the light of the aster, and the aerial capstone had to appear inaccessible.

The pyramid of Khafre
It dates back to 2520 B.C. It is 446 ft. tall (originally, it was 469 ft.) with a base of 689 x 689 ft. The top of the pyramid still has the original Tura outer limestone casing.

The Great Pyramid
It is the pyramid of Khufu, second pharaoh of the 4th Dynasty, built around 2550 B.C. It had been built with almost 2,500,000 compact limestone blocks, each one averaging about 2.5 tons. Its measurements exceed by a few yards those of the pyramid of Khafre.

KHAFRE'S CONSTRUCTION SITE
The stone blocks came from Aswan's quarries. Including the transport operations, the site should have stretched more than 497 miles across the entire Upper Egypt.

Chain work
All the work, extraction and transportation of the stone blocks, squaring, set up, and setting these in place, was carried out as chain work to avoid pauses.

The pyramid builders

So that the whole country might benefit from the pharaoh's divine power, even after his "earthly" death, many men steadily participated in the construction of the pyramids.

Referring to Khufu's colossal funerary monument, Herodotus mentioned that 100,000 men worked for twenty years without interruption in three-month turns. It still boggles the imagination to imagine how almost 3,000,000 cubic meters of stones, each weighing over two tons, were hauled and perfectly set into place at a height of almost 492 feet. The feat seems especially amazing in an age when iron, the wheel, the pul-

The ramps
To raise the pyramid, the builders used large raising ramps, along which enormous squared stone blocks were hauled by means of sleds on rollers.

Giza
The complex of Giza, southwest of Cairo, with the pyramids of Menkaure (on the left), Khafre, and Khufu.

ley, and the winch were unknown, and experts are still debating about how this was done. One hypothesis is that temporary rising ramps of various types were used; and another is that levers made from small beams hauled squared stone blocks from one level to another of the load-bearing step-sided structure of the construction. The Great Pyramids are marvelous creations of man—from the lowliest worker to the highest priest architect, designer, and chief engineer, all were gifted with extraordinary expertise and skill. Indeed, the accomplishment was so extraordinary that it was not continued beyond 2700–2500 B.C. It was as though these last formidable efforts exhausted whatever magic the Egyptians had used to build the structures.

A LONG EVOLUTION
The Egyptian funerary monument is the product of a very long evolution: from the simple mastabas to the pure geometry of the Giza Pyramids, though some designs attempted often failed.

The step pyramid
A series of step-sided mastabas, one on top of another, form the pyramid of the Pharaoh Zoser at Saqqara. It has a base of 397 X 358 ft. and a height of 197 ft.

The mastaba
It is the oldest type of Egyptian burial monument. This one-floor building has slightly bent external walls.

The true pyramid
It is the form of the Pyramid of Khufu, the tallest of the three Giza pyramids. Its base measures 755 X 755 ft. and its height 468 ft.

The bent pyramid
The Pyramid of Snefru at Dahshur presents a shift in the slope of the angle: from 54°27' in the lower part to 43°22' in the upper part. It has a base of 617 X 617 ft. and a height of 318 ft.

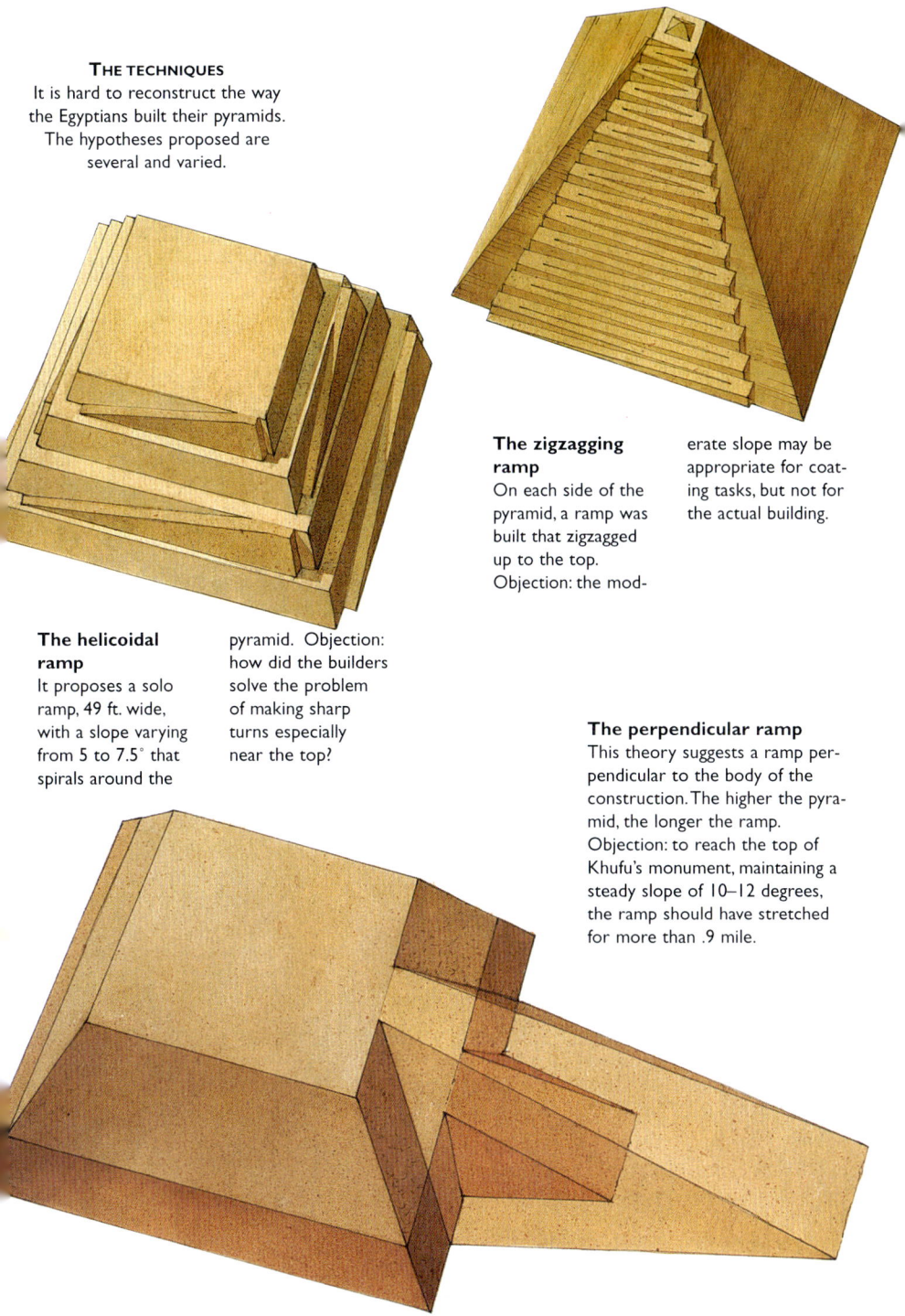

THE TECHNIQUES
It is hard to reconstruct the way the Egyptians built their pyramids. The hypotheses proposed are several and varied.

The zigzagging ramp
On each side of the pyramid, a ramp was built that zigzagged up to the top. Objection: the moderate slope may be appropriate for coating tasks, but not for the actual building.

The helicoidal ramp
It proposes a solo ramp, 49 ft. wide, with a slope varying from 5 to 7.5° that spirals around the pyramid. Objection: how did the builders solve the problem of making sharp turns especially near the top?

The perpendicular ramp
This theory suggests a ramp perpendicular to the body of the construction. The higher the pyramid, the longer the ramp. Objection: to reach the top of Khufu's monument, maintaining a steady slope of 10–12 degrees, the ramp should have stretched for more than .9 mile.

The mystery of the Sphinx

The "sphinx," a statue with a human head and lion's body, evolved during the reign of Zedefra, Khafre's immediate predecessor. The combination of human features and animal traits in a rounded sculpture of colossal dimensions is still inexplicable. No Old Kingdom document explains its religious significance. Perhaps, with its appearance of a crouching lion, the Sphinx was to watch over the pyramids' funerary complex. Its face seems to resemble that of the Pharaoh Khafre. It is a figure rich in symbolism. The king, who in many pre-dynastic paintings was portrayed as a lion wreaking havoc among his enemies, is again represented as one on the threshold of his afterlife dominion. Only a thousand years later, the statue started to be identified with Harmakhis (Horus at the horizon). When General Napoleon Bonaparte arrived in Egypt, only the head of the Sphinx, its neck, and a small part of its shoulders were visible above the sand. French scholars, and other Europeans, too, who still knew nothing of Egyptian history and culture, saw in the huge head a zodiacal representation of the "virgin."

The work to clear the sand that covered the Sphinx started in 1816. It continued, after an interruption in 1853, under the direction of Auguste Mariette and was completed in 1866. It was discovered that other efforts of the same kind had been carried out in earlier epochs. Between the mighty front legs of the Sphinx, a stele was found (still in place today) placed during the New Kingdom by Thutmose IV,

The giant that emerges from the sand
The Great Sphinx appeared like that to the French expeditionary force attached to Napoleon's army. This drawing was lished in the monumer *Description de l'Égypte.*

The Sphinx
The face of the Sphinx conveys precise information: scanty traces of color suggest that the majestic statue was originally fully painted.

Living statue
Sphinx is a Greek term derived from the Egyptian *shespankh*, or "living statue." The gigantic sculpture, carved from a natural mound of soft sandstone, is 240 ft. long and 66 ft. tall.

pharaoh of the Eighteenth Dynasty, of whom little is known. Ancient texts mention that the god Horus appeared to the king while he was asleep and asked him to dig out the sand that was covering it.

Paradoxically, attempts to restore the statue have endangered its survival. Now exposed to the air, its lion body is seriously menaced: accumulated salts from the ancient mortar cause further erosion when they melt from the humidity that comes from the base and dries out under the sun and the wind. The absence of the nose that gives to the Sphinx its hallmark expression of imperturbability is attributed to the artillery of the Mameluke soldiers. Some parts of the nose are now at the Museum of Cairo.

THE FIRST INTERMEDIATE PERIOD

At the end of the Sixth Dynasty, Ma'at's rule of order, safety, and harmony seemed to fall apart, and the old centralized system collapsed in general chaos. Periods of famine due to the meager flow of the Nile aggravated the situation.

At the end of the Old Kingdom, the administrative decentralization of Pepi II resulted in the steady erosion of the king's power. Formerly sovereign's representatives, governors became local princes and caused a crisis in the monarchy that plagued the pharaohs from the Seventh to the Eleventh Dynasty. This was the troubled time of the First Intermediate period, which began after 2200 B.C. and lasted between one hundred to one hundred ninety years, according to the calculations of scholars. A few difficult-to-interpret documents reveal that some governors, especially those of Edfu, Thebes, and Heracleopolis, fought each other with their private armies. They crowned them-

The beer
A small model reproducing women who filter big pieces of barley bread to prepare beer.

The bread
The grinding of the wheat in a little statue of 2200 B.C. To grind cereals, stone pestles and millstones were used.

selves kings and formed their own dynasties with succession rights for their family members. The situation worsened when tribes of eastern nomads, looking for new and richer grazing lands, invaded the Delta. Evidence of this event is the shifting of princes' tombs from Memphis, where the kings' power had diminished. They were subsequently spread everywhere across Upper Egypt, from Aswan to Thebes, and Abydos. At this time, too, the tombs began to be built in rocky areas, and were no longer characterized by the sumptuous grandiosity that celebrated the pharaoh's divinity and his status as the only one (with his retainers) who would reach the afterlife. The presence of numerous minor burials, or simply a stele, proved that the rich now felt entitled to an everlasting life, which in turn revealed changes in the social structure. Nonetheless, the disorder and anarchy did not stop pharaohs' construction of large works. Kheti III cut canals to link Memphis to other centers of the Delta. Mentuhotep I and, later, Mentuhotep II (who started the process of reunification of the country) equipped the Nile-Red Sea road with pits along the wadi to reach the region's gold mines and basalt quarries. The anarchy of this period did not result in decadence. The new grandees or noblemen were very clever administrators who brought a remarkable economic boom to their areas. Although visual arts and architecture decayed, literature flourished. It expressed nostalgia for the lost splendor and displayed a sense of pessimism born out of miseries and uncertainties.

A lyrical composition of this period, *The Harper's Song*, is among the most perfect creations of all time.

The monarch who reunified Egypt
Menthu-Hotep II carved in a static position. It is a sign of continuity and a tribute that the artist wants to pay to the Old Kingdom's art.

Fresco from the tomb of Iti
(Around 2100 B.C.) In the tomb of this prince of the First Intermediate period the sacrifice of an ox is painted with vivid simplicity.

Sculpture
It loses concern for portrayal of royal power. Common subjects prevail, as seen in the little statue reproducing a peasant carrying an ox on his shoulders.

THE MIDDLE KINGDOM

The events that had caused the collapse of the Old Kingdom did not eliminate the idea of a centralized power. However, the new pharaohs never regained the absolute control of the state that their predecessors, the kings of the Old Kingdom, had enjoyed.

The unification of Egypt, begun by Menthu-Hotep II around 2050 B.C., ended with the Theban princes of the Twelfth Dynasty. During the Middle Kingdom (1990–1785 B.C.), Thebes, in Upper Egypt, became the nominal capital of the country, although the pharaohs preferred to sojourn in different towns near the Faiyum. Apparently, the population did not grow dramatically during this period. The seven kings of this dynasty directed their efforts towards three well-defined goals. First, they challenged the power of the local princes in order to re-establish the pyramidal state. Second, they aimed at increasing their means and resources by

THE DELTA REGION
It is this bridging area that, after centuries of isolation, acts as a crossroad with other countries. It is also the door to invasions.

Memphis
Although no longer the capital, its geographical location on the Delta greatly favors its economy.

The frontier
The Delta's western branches deter Libyan raids.

The Mediterranean coast
Shallow and marshy, it does not offer landing possibilities. Vessels going to Egypt have to sail up the Delta to Memphis.

The good land
Works of drainage and reclamation have added more tillable land, together with rich grazing lands and fields.

financing extensive works of drainage and exploiting new mines. Third, they tried to bring affairs in the Levant, the Syrian coast, under Egyptian leadership so that they could better control the trade routes of the eastern Mediterranean. The dynasty was successful in reaching its goals. Under Sesostris III (1878–42 B.C.), district governors appointed by the monarch had already replaced the local nobility so that the administration was under royal control. Extensive areas of the Faiyum were fertilized and cultivated. Moreover, troops drawn from across Egypt subdued the northern region of Nubia, the gold mine country.

At the same time, the old Egyptian contacts with the Levant, with its center in Byblos, was reestablished and trade with Crete was peacefully intensified. To protect the borders, the pharaohs built a series of walled forts along the Suez line and others along the frontier with Nubia. The Middle Kingdom was a balanced age during which Amon, the Theban deity, became a dynastic god and received great honors.

A refined culture evolved, tinged with a certain pessimism towards human life. Although archeological marvels had almost completely crumbled away, superb masterpieces of statuary art remained. This art underwent a big change. In the pharaoh's rep-

Goods from the Levant
An Asian nomad loading a donkey with goods to bring to Egypt.

Amenemhet III
Sixth pharaoh of the 12th Dynasty, he ruled during the Middle Kingdom from 1842 to 1797 B.C.

Sesostris I
Realistic portrait of the second pharaoh of the 12th Dynasty, who ruled from 1961 to 1928 B.C.

resentations, the Middle Kingdom no longer exudes its typical self-assurance. A more thoughtful approach seemed to stress a different concept of power. The events of the First Intermediate period had taught a lesson. Weaknesses in the king's divine authority had been revealed. The monarch learned the need to know his people better and to know how to rule them well.

Foreign markets

During the Middle Kingdom, flourishing craftsmanship matched bountiful farming production (grain, linen, and papyrus), which together promoted the rise of a middle class. The Egypt of the Middle Kingdom not only had an agricultural surplus, but also an abundance of artifacts for which there was insufficient internal demand, especially for valuable goods (gems, ointments, perfumes, gold jewels, animal hides, and refined wooden objects).

This overproduction in agriculture and craftsmanship could only have been absorbed by trade with other countries, in particular the lands of the Levant and Minoan Crete. Phoenician

The round boat
The Phoenician boat is wide and has a double curved prow. It is built for long trips across the Mediterranean.

The Minoans
Their flat vessels have a very long prow and a double sail attached to a unique mast.

The tribute
All the arriving goods belonged to the pharoah and were declared before the scribe of the port who recieved a tax in gold or in kind.

vessels distributed the exquisite Egyptian goods to all the ports of the Mediterranean and in exchange brought Spanish tin, timber, and silver to Egypt. From Crete, which controlled the islands of the Aegean Sea, the Egyptians imported wine, oil, and decorative art. To intensify this trade, the

The Phoenicians
Their boats have characteristic horse-head prows.

THE PORT
Boats anchored in a Delta harbor. The first trading exchanges are made directly on the docksides where debarking sailors swap their wages (in grain, wine, or oil) for garments, fruit, and vegetables.

73

Egyptians allowed permanent Phoenician, Minoan, and Syrian trading posts to be stationed on the Delta.

The Faiyum

The Middle Kingdom's pharaohs involved themselves with extensive works of drainage to increase farming land along the banks of the Nile. To do this, Sesostris II and his successors devised a large project. The Bahr Yusef was dammed to regulate the downflow of the great marshy Lake Moeris, located in the Faiyum depression. Thanks to a well-planned network of canals, a vast farming area around it was fertilized, and today it is still one of the

A STATUS SYMBOL: THE VILLA
An estate in the Faiyum is a social status symbol. Other than the pharaoh and the members of the royal family, few other nobles can afford it. Each plot costs more than a house in Thebes.

On the roof
For the children and servants of the farm, the flat roof is a place of enjoyment and relaxation. People work under the shelter, play ball games, and cool themselves with water from a well provided by a servant.

country's most productive areas.

The Faiyum Oasis soon attracted many new colonists. Villages, big farms, temples dedicated to Sobek, the local crocodile-headed god, and grand mansions rose, where even pharaohs loved to pass their time. The pharaohs decided to build their tombs nearby, again shaped as pyramids (now ingeniously built with a combination of bricks and stones) with an annexed temple. This return to the old customs seemed to reflect the order regained in the internal affairs after the chaos of the First Intermediate period.

In the holiday villa

During the Middle Kingdom in this

An immense back garden
The division into orderly, irrigated fields allows the cultivation of any kind of vegetables, such as lettuce, onions, chickpeas, broad beans, melons, and lentils, on a vast scale. If the valley is the silo of Egypt, the Faiyum is its back garden.

THE LANDSCAPE
A plain shining with colors: the azure of Lake Moeris, the green of bushy palms and grass, the reddish-brown of the freshly ploughed soil, and, here and there, the striking white of the farms' plastered walls.

fashionable region, huge estates developed that were both farms and residential villas. The farm area, formed by various courts, included silos, an underground basement, stables with rooms for butchering animals, workrooms, a household brewery, and work stations for potters and carpenters. There were also kitchen gardens, pens for the geese, washing areas, an oven, and a big well for the water. The typical one-floor rectangular villa had a lavish reception area with an entrance hall, vestibule, living room, and internal courtyards and a series of smaller rooms where people lived containing a bathroom, a toilet, a dining room, hallways, bedrooms, and a workroom. A vast garden with trees, terraces, and pools, surrounded the public area of the house and was integrated with it. It was here, more than inside, where the social life was found. The Egyptians loved to show off the way they enjoyed their wealth more than they loved their wealth itself. To live in a villa meant to have prestige, that is, to host guests, entertain them, offer banquets and diversions, all done with elegance, gusto, balance, and refinement.

Nubia

Besides the Faiyum, other new lands attracted the Egyptians: those of Nubia, known as Ta-setj, "the arch country," very likely a reference to Nubian archers. However, for the Egyptians of the Middle Kingdom and following periods, Nubia was the country of gold, ivory, and mercenary soldiers.

The Egyptians considered the lands

THE PARTY IS ON
At sunset, host and villa guests moved to the garden around the water-lily pools, and decorative fruit trees.

Board games
In a quiet corner, some guests sit around the checkerboard moving the thin ivory sticks of the game "the dog and the jackal." Bets can escalate.

The show
Music and dance entertain the guests. Draped in veils and garlands, dancers gracefully undulate to the notes of harp, lyre, and double flute.

The banquet
Meatloaves, grilled oxen and geese, fish from the lake, fruit and vegetables from the kitchen garden, sweets made with dates and carobs, and wine and beer for everybody.

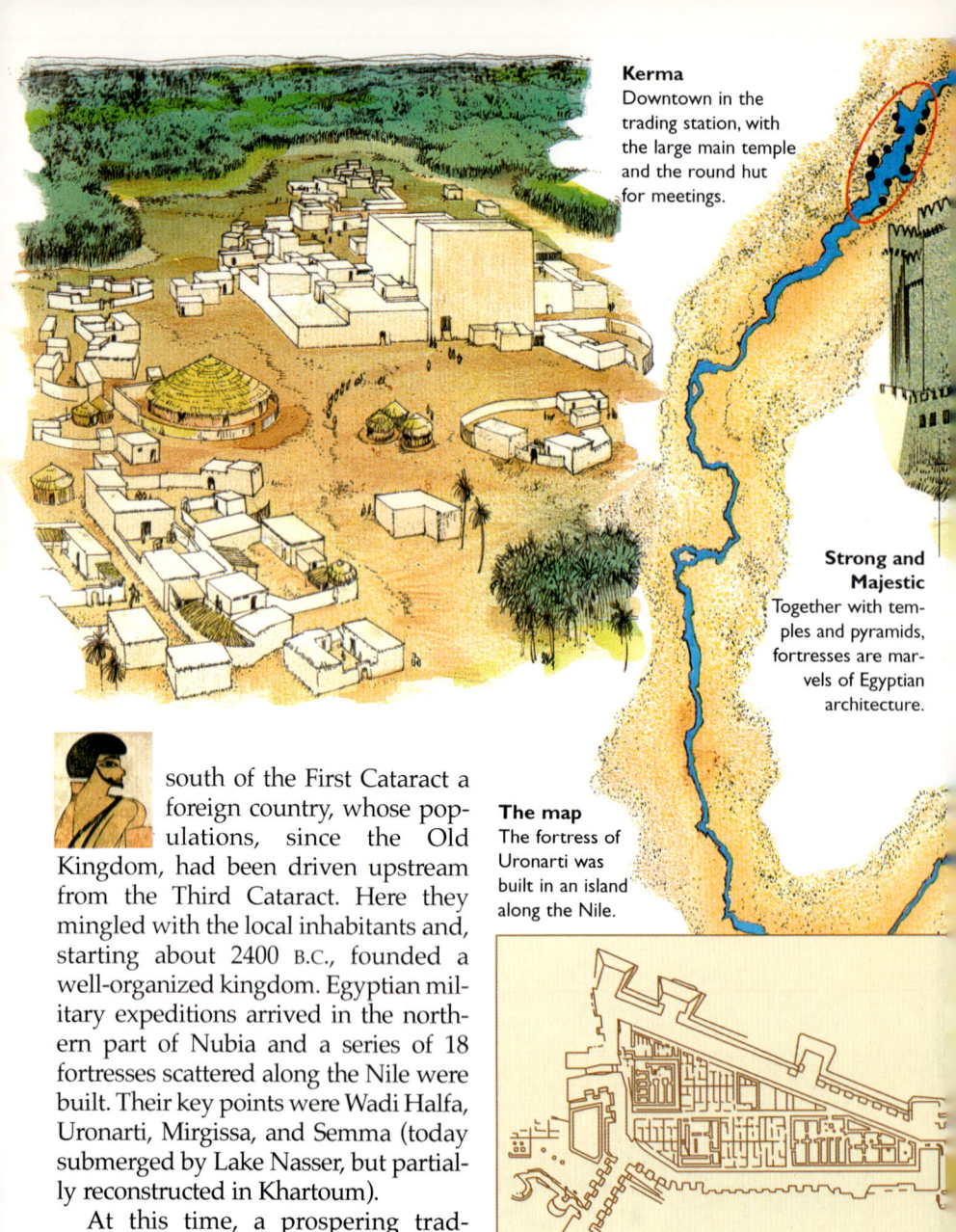

Kerma
Downtown in the trading station, with the large main temple and the round hut for meetings.

Strong and Majestic
Together with temples and pyramids, fortresses are marvels of Egyptian architecture.

The map
The fortress of Uronarti was built in an island along the Nile.

south of the First Cataract a foreign country, whose populations, since the Old Kingdom, had been driven upstream from the Third Cataract. Here they mingled with the local inhabitants and, starting about 2400 B.C., founded a well-organized kingdom. Egyptian military expeditions arrived in the northern part of Nubia and a series of 18 fortresses scattered along the Nile were built. Their key points were Wadi Halfa, Uronarti, Mirgissa, and Semma (today submerged by Lake Nasser, but partially reconstructed in Khartoum).

At this time, a prospering trading station was opened in Kerma, in southern Nubia, which was still an independent region.

Wadi Halfa
Built entirely with unbaked bricks during the reign of Sesostris I, the fort is rectangular, has external crenellated walls 13 ft. deep and 16½ ft. high, from which semicircular ramparts emerge. It follows an internal fortification 33 ft. high with square ramparts.

FRONTIER WAR
It seems that the Egyptians did not have any siege machinery. Egyptians resorted to swift and violent sorties.

Gold and prestige
Nubian regions offer few farming opportunities, but its conquest brings gold and ivory to Egypt, along with increased military prestige, necessary to strengthen the unity of the country.

THE SECOND INTERMEDIATE PERIOD

Unification did not last long, and a new crisis followed. We do not know what caused this second period of upheaval. During this transitional period, the country was split and underwent foreign domination and a war of liberation.

Egypt's riches attracted new goods and peaceful foreign delegates, but its economic success also brought dissent within. In 1786 B.C., with the end of the Twelfth Dynasty and of the Middle Kingdom, the Second Intermediate period began, which was a tormented and obscure age in Egyptian history that lasted until 1570 B.C. Egypt split again with a Thirteenth Dynasty in the south and a Fourteenth Dynasty co-regent in the north.

Probably, following a system of royal grants similar to the one that had caused the end of the Old Kingdom, local regencies arose and the Syrian and Nubian empires everywhere broke away. This division weakened Egypt so much that it was unable to mount a strong defense against eastern invaders. Periodically, for centuries, nomads had filtered into the Delta, across the harsh regions of Sinai, in search of grazing lands for their cattle. They had long been tolerated because they

NEW PEOPLE
Small caravans of herdsmen grow bigger and bigger at Egypt's eastern border, asking to settle in the rich grazing lands of the Delta.

worked hard and sought little. The collapse of centralized power gave free reign to these nomads. Their infiltration turned into an armed invasion.

The Hyksos invade Egypt

Around 2000 B.C. huge migrations from the north upset the equilibrium of the Levant. This migration wave brought bands of Canaanite nomads into Egypt, following trade routes. The Egyptians called them Hyksos, (*hik-khase*), or "foreign chieftains." About 1640 B.C. the Hyksos were in the lead. Neither herdsmen nor disorganized marauders, but true warriors, they mastered a weapon unknown in the Nile Valley: war chariots drawn by

Free entrance for peaceful immigrants
Egypt welcomes workers. Every newcomer, however, must be counted and recorded by the scribes.

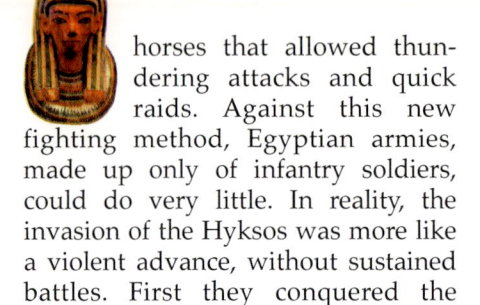

horses that allowed thundering attacks and quick raids. Against this new fighting method, Egyptian armies, made up only of infantry soldiers, could do very little. In reality, the invasion of the Hyksos was more like a violent advance, without sustained battles. First they conquered the Eastern Delta, where they founded their own capital, Avaris. They ruled over Egypt, subjugating the local princes as tributaries. Hyksos rulers did not want merely to exploit or rob the country. They wanted to live well in their conquered land and become its citizens. They created their own dynasties.

Tributaries
The Hyksos did not get rid of the native defeated sovereigns. They subdued them, however, demanding tributes from them.

Chariot troops
War chariots clashed with the Egyptian infantry soldiers, disbanding them. Then, quickly, the Hyksos chase and attack the dismantled and terrified regiments.

A new animal: the horse
The Egyptians knew only one equine: the donkey. They had used it as a beast of burden, but not for pulling. They soon loved horses so much that they later used them to dislodge the Hyksos.

Quickly, they succeeded in establishing contacts with Nubian kings, signing alliances with local princes who escaped their control. The Theban kings were under strict control and rebelled around 1600 B.C. A war of liberation followed, begun by Kamose, the last pharaoh of the Seventeenth Dynasty, and ended in 1552 B.C. when Ahmose founded the native Eighteenth Dynasty. During the period of the Hyksos domination, possibly the Israelites, decendants of Abraham, immigrated into Egypt and remained for the next 300 years.

THE NEW KINGDOM

This was the height of Egyptian civilization. During the New Kingdom, Egypt came out of its isolation and became an important player in international political affairs. To do this, it had to fight against the armies of the Near East, which were very well trained.

The New Kingdom (1552–1084 B.C.) was Egypt's period of highest glory and accomplishment in Egypt's history. It began when the war of liberation against the Hyksos ended. The population then numbered between five and eight million. The pharaohs carried out an imperialist policy outside the borders of the country, subduing nearby populations and forming political alliances and dynasties with the great states that had been forming in Anatolia and Mesopotamia (the Babylonian, Assyrian, and Hittite empires). It also established a wide network of commercial trades with all the Eastern Mediterranean countries, upon which a great part of the welfare of Egypt depended. The politics of expansion started with Thutmose I, third pharaoh of the Eighteenth Dynasty, who took possession of another part of the Nubia up to the Fourth Cataract and delegated the government to a viceroy (a figure who at this point

Abu Simbel
One of the colossi's heads from the façade of the temple of Ramses II, cut into the cliffs at Abu Simbel.

THE HEART OF THE EMPIRE
Although imperialistic wars are fought in the north, the halfway point of the Nile remained the core of Egypt's religious and political life. For a short period, El-Amarna deprived Thebes of its role as capital. Abu Simbel remained the door to Nubia.

Tell el-Amarna
A bust of Queen Nefertiti, discovered in the new capital founded by Akhenaten.

Thebes
Ruins of the funerary temple of Ramses II, known as Ramesseum, west of Thebes.

appears for the first time in Egyptian history). After the death of his successor, Thutmose II, an extraordinary and unique event happened at the top of the Egyptian hierarchy: a woman pharaoh, Hatshepsut, ascended the throne. She ruled the country for twenty prosperous and peaceful years in her own name until the succession of her stepson Thutmose III, who claimed the throne in 1490 B.C. With him, perhaps the greatest pharaoh in all Egyptian history, imperial conquests expanded Egyptian territory to its maximum, especially along the eastern borders. After having defeated a coalition of Palestinian and Phoenician towns in a great battle at Megiddo, Thutmose III conducted seventeen military campaigns in Asia, conquering Phoenician cities and marching beyond the Euphrates River. For the first time, an Egyptian pharaoh had become a leader of international affairs. The entire Near East paid homage to him and to his immediate successors: Amenhotep II, Thutmose IV, and Amenhotep III. The prestige of the dynasty also grew because of wisely arranged marriages with foreign princesses. During this period, Egyptian supremacy

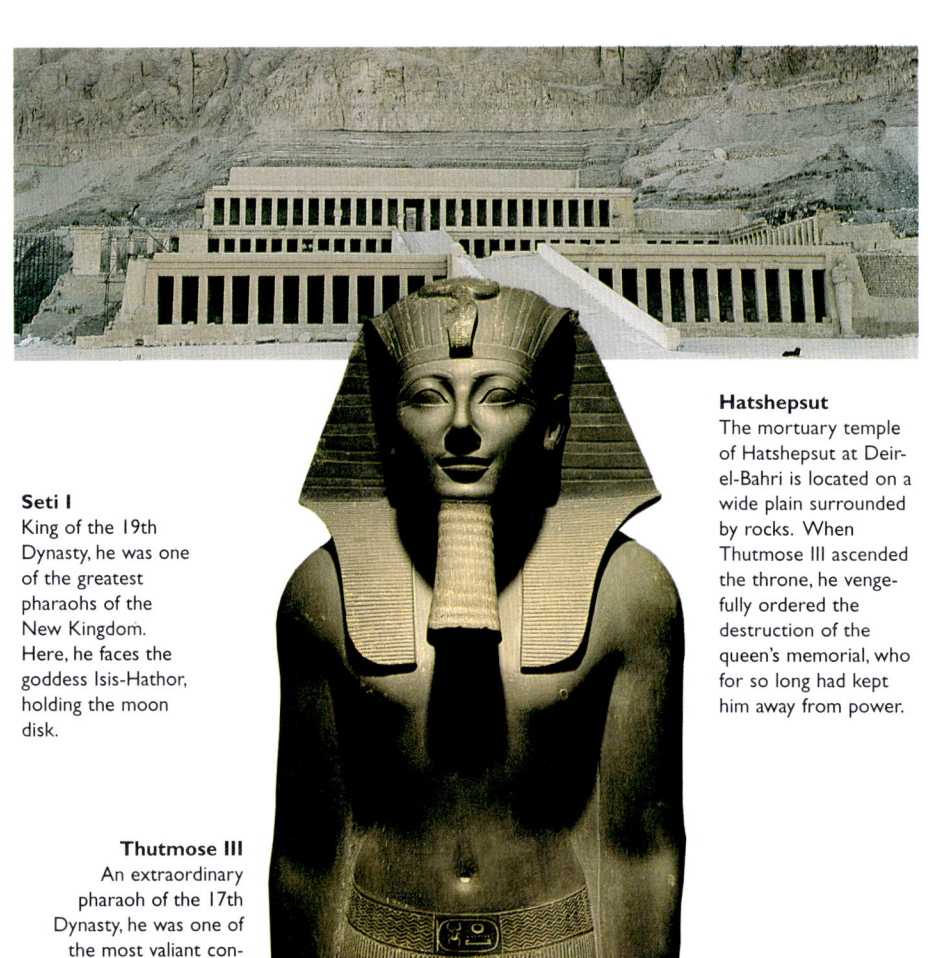

Seti I
King of the 19th Dynasty, he was one of the greatest pharaohs of the New Kingdom. Here, he faces the goddess Isis-Hathor, holding the moon disk.

Hatshepsut
The mortuary temple of Hatshepsut at Deir-el-Bahri is located on a wide plain surrounded by rocks. When Thutmose III ascended the throne, he vengefully ordered the destruction of the queen's memorial, who for so long had kept him away from power.

Thutmose III
An extraordinary pharaoh of the 17th Dynasty, he was one of the most valiant conquerors of antiquity.

extended over Cyprus and Crete. However, the pharaoh Amenhotep IV jeopardized everything by rejecting the military uniform in favor of the sacred vestment.

Thebes, a busy capital

Thebes was again the capital of imperialist Egypt. Here the king lived surrounded by an administrative apparatus organized on a pyramidal scheme. The city attracted not only priests, officials, and military personnel, whose numbers were growing because of the many military expeditions, but also anyone wishing to ascend the social ladder who was eager to profit from the opportunities offered by an expanding empire. Compared to the past, the entry of capable individuals into top civil positions increased the social mobility of the Old Egypt. By favoring trades and production proper to state capitalism, this middle class made the city quite wealthy. At this time, too, Thebes became the artistic and cultural center of Egypt.

The main and oldest part of town stretched along the eastern bank of the Nile, around the big temple complexes of Luxor and Karnak dedicated to the cult of Amon, the local god. These temple complexes were the symbols of the New Kingdom, just as the pyramids of Memphis were the hallmarks of the Old Kingdom.

On the opposite bank (west of Thebes), villages of workers and free

THE CITY OF AMON
The Egyptians of the New Kingdom called their capital *Niut-Amon*, from which the biblical name of Thebes derives.

The roads
They were narrow and crowded as in other villages.

Houses
There were neither rich nor poor quarters. A house could have one or more floors. The roof was flat and the windows were barred with wooden trellises that were no more than air and light openings to let a cool breeze filter in.

At the market
Here, the fish of the Nile and produce arriving daily from the country are bartered. Cattle were also traded.

peasants spread out over the countryside. Farther on, along the steep coastline, funerary temples and cemeteries of pharaohs and their wives were located. In this way, the slow-moving Nile divided the world of the living from the world of the dead.

The court

The "Great House" was both a dwelling place and a palace of ceremonies, where the pharaoh lived with his family and courtiers. Among his family members were three types of queens (the "king's mother," the "king's wives," and the "king's great wife," who was the heirs' mother) and the concubines with their children. There were also the king's relatives, considered intimate friends of the pharaoh, the children of allied

The symbols
Both the blue crown and the crook that the pharaoh holds in his right hand are symbols of power. He holds the ankh cross in his left hand, the symbol of the life that he has the power of giving or taking.

THE RITUAL
Every act of the pharaoh is a display. The god turns towards his people.

The tribute
All the grand court dignitaries, and wives and concubines of the Great House kneel respectfully before the triumphant pharaoh, whom they obediently serve.

The court
The pharaoh, majestic in his palanquin, escorts food offerings and gifts to the temples, presented each day to the divinity.

sovereigns used by Thebes as hostages, and a few officials who had distinguished themselves in military campaigns or had proven themselves indispensable in business.

The court included servants attending the royal highnesses (butlers, waiters, hairdressers, perfumers, manicurists, and doctors) and the artisans working for them (sculptors, carpenters, goldsmiths, and tailors). There were also noblewomen, wives of high-ranking officers, who formed a guild under the protection of Hathor, the cow-goddess and foster-mother of kings. The pharaoh was a distant and untouchable person, even

Faïence
The Egyptians did not know about blown or pure glass, only of a glass paste, called faïence, from which they made strings or threads to wrap around a core of terra cotta.

Market objects
Bright decorations as well as religious and magic glass paste symbols are even found on everyday objects.

Master "glass-makers"
They melt a mix of silica powders, lime, sodium carbonate, potassium carbonate, and lead in big refractory pots.

for the courtiers who competed among themselves for his slightest attention. The god-king kept his subjects at a rigorous distance and appeared in public only during important ceremonies, regulated by rigid rituals.

The development of craftsmanship

The situation of the artisans changed significantly during the New Kingdom. They formed a middle class that was well integrated into the economic life of the country, although the court or the temple, as before, continued to hire many of them. The working techniques of some artisans changed or evolved because of external influences. Contacts with other civilizations and popula-

Pottery
Vases, amulets, and small statues are covered with glass paste, decorated with threads of different colors, and cooked for a long time in ovens burning at very high temperatures.

A refined artisan
Cosmetic pots: a highly demanded export article.

tions annexed to the empire made Egyptians aware of new materials and, thus, of new manufacturing techniques. One of these materials was iron, learned from the Hittites during the campaign of Thutmose III and his successors, another was glass paste from Phoenicia and Mesopotamia.

The temple

The temple for the cult, the house of the god and the pharaohs, was located at the center of a group of buildings. Its structure was constantly the same, as it was said that the gods themselves had designed it in all its details, even the size of the walls. In each temple's highest and darkest point was the sanctuary, the place where the *ka* (or the spirit) of the divinity appeared, evoked by the statue hidden in the shrine. In theory, only the king could face the god. In reality, he delegated his duties to the main priest or "first servant of god." Other priests worked under the main priest's orders (file clerks, scholars of ancient texts, administrators), together with artisans and peasants. After the Middle Kingdom, when the number of priestly privileges had decreased, the temples again owned huge estates, often tax-exempt by royal decree, which produced grain, fruit, and vegetables and raised cattle for the god and the people serving the cult.

By 1250 B.C., during the reign of

KARNAK
It is the sacred region of Thebes where Amon had its main temple. Originally, it was a modest complex, but later, due to the additions made by New Kingdom pharaohs, it took on gigantic proportions.

The map
The Temple of Amon was enlarged repeatedly until it assumed a very complex structure.

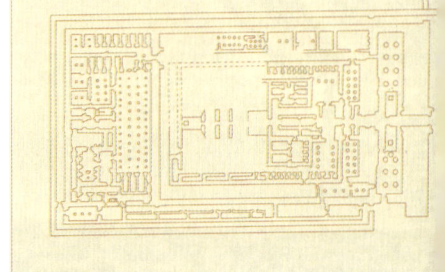

The container
When proceeding towards the rear of the Egyptian temple, the level of the ground rises and the height of the roof decreases so as to create an impression of warmth and waiting.

The naos
It is the shrine that hosts and hides the god's statue. Lateral rooms, where the goods of the temple are kept, encompass it.

The central aisle
It is open with columns arranged around the walls. An external pylon door provides access.

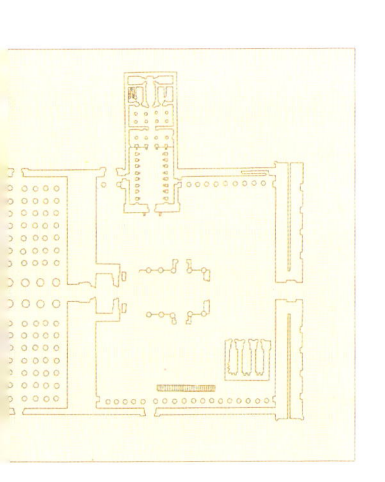

Luxor
Bound to the Karnak complex from the processional boulevard of the Sphinxes, it contains the temple of Amenhotep III, famous for its splendid columns shaped like closed lotus flowers.

The colossi of Memnon
They are monolithic statues of quartzite, almost 50 ft. high. It is all that remains of the funerary temple of Amenhotep III, built west of Thebes.

Ramses II, more than 80 thousand men were working in the temple of Karnak, along with 400 thousand cattle. The high priests of Thebes became so powerful that they even took civil positions that they were entitled to pass on to their heirs. This led to constant tensions between the monarchy and the clergy of Amon, who practically constituted an autonomous church-state.

The ceremonies

Only priests of higher ranks could approach the statue of the god, to which they brought food and drinks three times a day. The high priest or, if he was present, the king unlatched the door of the sanctuary and walked inside. First, he undressed the statue and cleaned it with water and natron (sodium carbonate solution), then he carefully smoothed paints along the god's eyes. Finally, he clothed the statue in clean linen. Then, pronouncing the ritual formulas, he invoked the *ka* and offered it the food and drink of the divine meal. Once the ceremony was over, the doors of the sanctuary were sealed with clay until the following meal, and the high priest took care to remove any traces of human presence by erasing the marks that he had left behind him on the sand floor. During the most important festivities, the statue of the god was placed on a ceremonial barge of gilded wood and carried on the shoulders of the priests along the perimeter of the temple's walls so that ordinary people could pay homage to it.

The high priest
He wears sacred vestments to perform his duty of satisfying the daily needs of the god, just as the chamberlain attends to the king at court.

The sanctuary
Inaccessible to everybody except the pharaoh and the high priests, it is not the richest and most glamorous part of the temple. The *ka* needs privacy and detachment.

The temple school

In every temple complex there was a school or "House of Life." It was the temple archive where religious and instructional texts, narrative essays, autobiographies, scientific treatises, and texts of astronomy and magic were copied, studied, and transmitted to future generations.

The "House of Life" was, therefore, similar to a school where observations noted across centuries and data collected by scholars were elaborated upon and used for new inquiries.

For the dead pharaohs
Food is also kept in the sanctuary for the god's meal. Afterwards, it will be offered to the dead pharaohs, whose names are chiseled on a wall in the back of the temple. They will be called one by one, except for Queen Hatshepsut, who has offended the gods.

THREE CALLS FOR THE *KA*
In the silence, in the most secretive dark area of the temple, the *ka* of the god is invoked three times a day, in the morning, at dusk, and in the evening, so that he feeds himself.

97

However, what could a medical student or a novice astronomer or a young literary student who hoped to make a career in the world of letters learn at the temple school? Medicine was strictly linked to religious practices and was based on rituals and codified formulas. Medical knowledge, however, was well advanced, as the *Ebers Medical Papyrus* shows. This is a compilation of medical cases in which the symptoms of illnesses are described. The heart was considered the center of life. Its beat was connected with the pulse. Surgery was known; the experience they acquired through mummification rendered the Egyptians experts on human anatomy. Cuts were stitched by burning the tissues with a hot iron or with caustic products and by applying stitches as a type of bandage. Anesthesia was obtained from the opium poppy.

As for literature, schools used the "wisdom texts." They were a series of sayings or teachings passed down from earlier epochs. They advised the reader about how to behave correctly in life. The oldest, but timeless, wisdom book found in the library of any temple was the *Instruction of the Vizier Ptahhotep* of the Old Kingdom, a "practical guide" to the success that people can attain with good education, a respect for social status, and moderation in life. Other famous examples of literature to leaf through and meditate upon were the already cited *Harper's Song*, the *Satire of the Trades*, and the famed *Story of Sinuhe*. Besides this intellectual

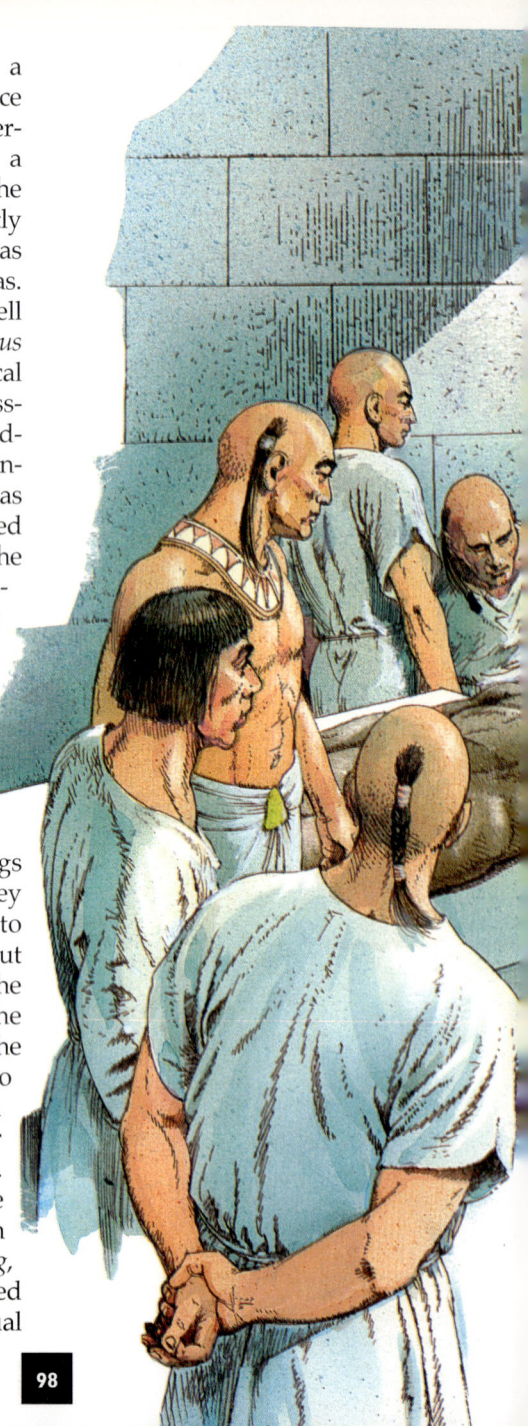

A modern method
Like their modern colleagues, Egyptian physicians recognized an illness based on its symptoms (diagnosis) and they forecasted its treatment and results (prognosis).

THE SCHOOL OF MEDICINE
At the temple school of medicine, highly specialized professionals taught. They were appreciated and even known abroad.

material, a literature that we would today call entertaining appeared during the New Kingdom. This consisted of humorous and grotesque stories, war chronicles (a classic in an expanding empire), and love songs, which find their most fertile ground in an epoch of abundance and social order.

The students who devoted themselves to the study of astronomy were the least fortunate. In this subject, the Egyptians never equaled their neighbors, the Sumerians and Babylonians, with whom they should have probably exchanged studies and information. The major contributions of the Egyptians to this subject were the division of the day and night into twelve equal parts and the solar calendar into 365 days. The observation of the stars taught them to distinguish between the mobile stars in the equatorial area, which they called "tireless," and those that were fixed circumpolar, which they called "eternal." Using both types of stars, they designated figures in human or animal shape (a sort of Zodiac) linked to mythology or religion.

This and much else could be learned in the *House of Life*, but theoretical instruction, then as now, was insufficient in itself. The prospective doctors applied their knowledge among the ranks of the imperial armies; the literate searched for a rich patron to flatter and amuse with their compositions; and most of the astronomers lost themselves in a labyrinth of theories.

In difficult times, there was always the possibility of remaining scribes or priests in the temple or in the sanctuary.

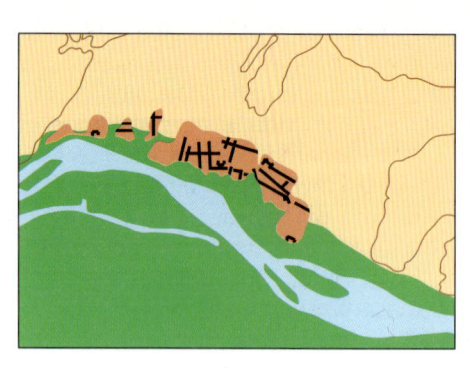

"The Horizon of Aton"
The map shows the former project of the town of Akhetaten. Today, only the barren contours of the walls remain.

Akhenaten
The fine features that enrich the face with a serene and forlorn expression belong to Akhenaten.

Their power was measured by the number of their disciples.

The religious crisis

Egypt had just reached its maximum splendor when the entire administrative structure was shaken by an abrupt religious crisis caused by King Amenhotep IV, manifested by a total lack of interest in the Egyptian Empire. During the second part of the Eighteenth Dynasty, the Theban sanctuary of Amon had reached a condition of such great importance and autonomy as to rival the state, especially because top civil positions were given to its high-ranking priests and because of the generous gifts of sovereigns. It was a dangerous situation that Amenhotep IV, who ruled from 1364 to 1381, tried to correct. He deprived the highest-ranking priest of Amon of his possessions and instituted a religious reform that shook the whole administrative structure. Amenhotep IV replaced the cult of Amon with that of Aton, a less-known divinity, represented by the sun disk conceived as a universal and beneficial force of nature.

The king also changed his name from Amenhotep ("Amon is benevolent") to that of Akhenaten ("He who serves Aton") and left Thebes to found the new capital Akhetaten ("The Horizon of Aton"), near the modern Tell el-Amarna (175 miles north of Thebes). However, a religious reform so profound did not agree with the feelings of a deeply traditional population. Such a strong opposition arose against it that Akhenaton's successors reinstated the state religion, allowing the worship of the old deities as well as Aton. Calm returned and Ramses II clashed with the Hittites for the control over the Syro-Palestinian region. Then he established a long period of peace between the two empires. The copious treasures captured from spoils of the victorious wars and regular tributes from the provinces were reflected by the richness of the funerary monuments and by temples of unprecedented grandeur. They arose all over the country and particularly in the splendid capital of Thebes. In about 1190, Ramses III of the Twentieth Dynasty saved the country

Towards Aton
The royal family of Tell el-Amarna turns to Aton who fills and sanctifies it with its luminous rays.

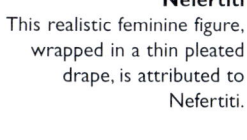

Nefertiti
This realistic feminine figure, wrapped in a thin pleated drape, is attributed to Nefertiti.

from a new external danger by defeating the Sea Peoples. Under his successors, however, internal riots eventually resulted in the loss of both Palestine and Nubia.

The Royal Valley

The successor of Akhenaten, his son-in-law Tutankhamen, had reinstalled the cult of Amon. Although he only reigned for a short period, he took on the role of Egypt's defender from external menaces and, with

The dream of every archeologist
On November 27, 1922, the British archeologist Howard Carter entered an undisturbed tomb of the 18th Dynasty. Three months were spent clearing the antechamber and a lateral small walled chamber. Then, the burial chamber was opened. It contained five chests, one on top of another. Inserted in the last one were three coffins. In the inner one, the body of the pharaoh Tutankhamen laid exactly as it had been placed thirty-three centuries before.

The mask
It is made of gold, inlaid with stripes of blue glass paste. It covered the face and the shoulders of Tutankhamen.

his generals, regained the country's positions in the Levant and in Nubia.

However, his fame is linked to his celebrated tomb, discovered in the Royal Valley on the plain between the Nile and the Libyan Desert. Thutmose I had been the first king to introduce this new type of royal tomb that was cut into the cliffs. That technique was to be

The treasure
In Tutankhamen's tomb, precious chests, a gold throne, vases of alabaster, gold heads of animals, items and objects of every kind were found, including two dismantled chariots.

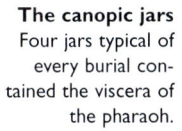

The canopic jars
Four jars typical of every burial contained the viscera of the pharaoh.

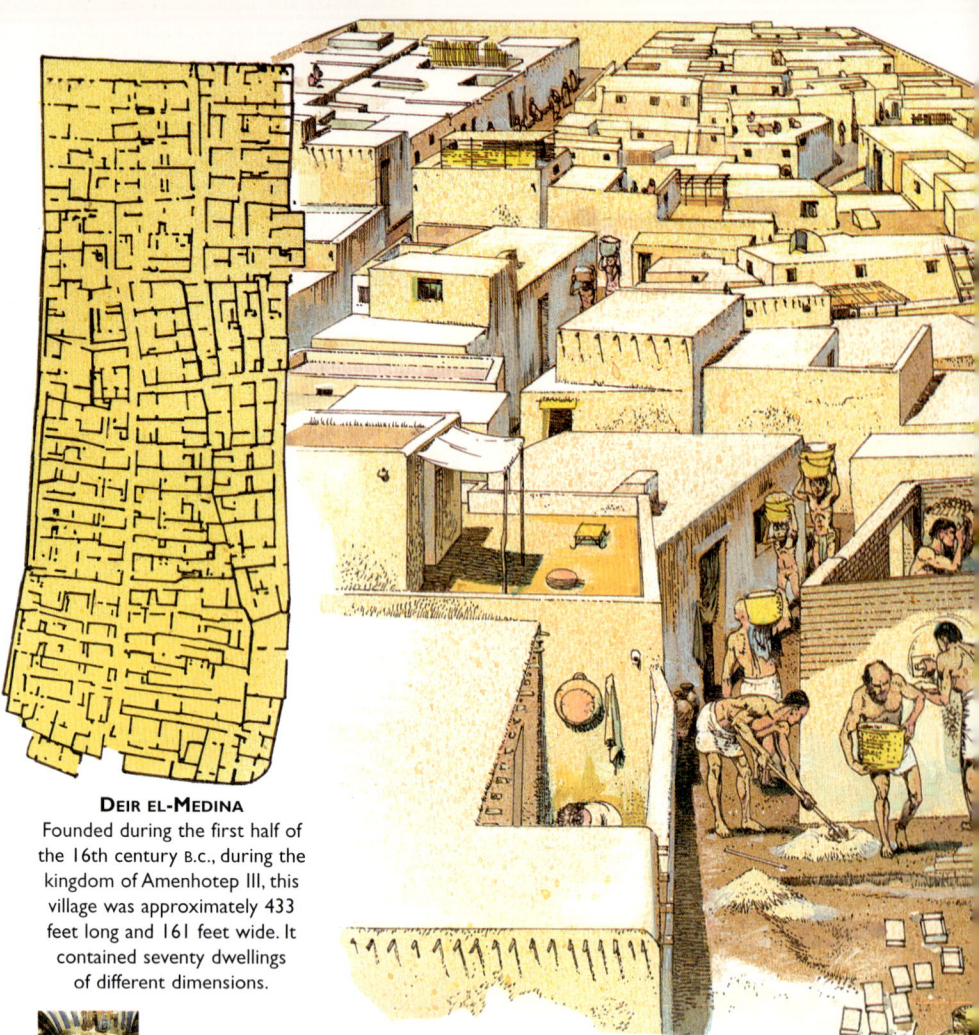

DEIR EL-MEDINA
Founded during the first half of the 16th century B.C., during the kingdom of Amenhotep III, this village was approximately 433 feet long and 161 feet wide. It contained seventy dwellings of different dimensions.

repeatedly used throughout the New Kingdom.

Far away and detached in the plateau, the barren Royal Valley, dominated by a mountain shaped like a pyramid called The Peak, is the site of some of the most famous monuments of the Nile Valley (The Temple of Queen Hatshepsut, the Ramesseum of Ramses II, and the Colossi of Memnon, portraying Amenhotep III on the throne). The rich burials of the sovereigns, nobles, and highest dignitaries were located in the least accessible areas of the valley. Their wives and cadet children were placed in the desolate Valley of the Queen, further southwest.

The workers village

The laborers and artists, who worked at the tombs of the Valley of the Kings, lived with their families in the village of Deir el-Medina, located in a lateral deep valley at the foot of the mountain. As the burials had to remain secret, the community was well supervised, and well supplied, but was kept apart. The village, which was surrounded by a massive mud-brick wall with only one entrance door, hosted more than 1,000 inhabitants, only some of which worked at the necropolis. Laborers, diggers, master masons, architects, sculptors, and painters were flanked by scribes who organized the work and also by chiefs of warehouses full of materials such as colored pigments, copper tools, and timber for the scaffoldings. There were also those charged with public

The houses
They were constructed of unbaked plastered brick, their floors were made of pounded earth, and the roof was flat. They were constructed in rows and each one housed a single family.

Two roads
The excavation shows a unique road that crosses the village lengthwise. A transverse road departs from it, going west.

From the model to the final product
Using the method of proportions, a few workers have divided the wall into squares in order to enlarge the contours of the model, which was previously sketched on a palette or a papyrus roll by the "painter scribe."

services, such as water carriers, herdsmen, women who cultivated wheat for the bread and barley for the beer. All the other foods, especially salt, came from outside and formed part of the workers' wages. Aware of their importance as builders of eternal dwellings, the workers of Deir el-Medina knew how to defend their rights. In extreme situations, they even went on strike. Before falling into the oblivion around 1080 B.C. and being buried in sand, Deir el-Medina had been a bustling village for almost 500 years.

The decorations of the royal tombs

In the tombs of the Valley of the

Kings, various laborers worked in tandem: while a team was busy digging, another one was already spreading the stucco on the walls upon which the painters reproduced the model sketched by an artist on a papyrus roll. The painting, which earlier epochs considered complementary to both sculpture and relief, stands out in the New Kingdom. Themes of religious subjects were practically compulsory, tied to century-old artistic traditions. However, greater freedom was granted to everyday representations, which were more realistic and livelier. For them, artists tried new solutions, such as the three-quarter view. Their subtle care for details gives us a precise source of information. Without the discovery of the tomb paintings, we would certainly know little or nothing of the garments, hairstyles, foods, tools, activities, and games of the refined civilization of Egypt.

Colors
Painting with tempera was accomplished by using basic tones made from different materials: black from carbon, white from chalk, blue from lapis lazuli, green from malachite, and red and yellow from ochre.

The canons of proportions
The human figure was enclosed by a grid 18 squares tall, which, from head to toe, contained the subject to be depicted. Two squares were needed for the face and neck; the outline of the sixth marked the waistline; hips and the pelvis occupied three spaces; and eight were reserved for the legs. A small square was for the palm of the hand and the fingers. The arm took five vertical spaces, the shoulders required six horizontal ones, and three squares were needed for the foot.

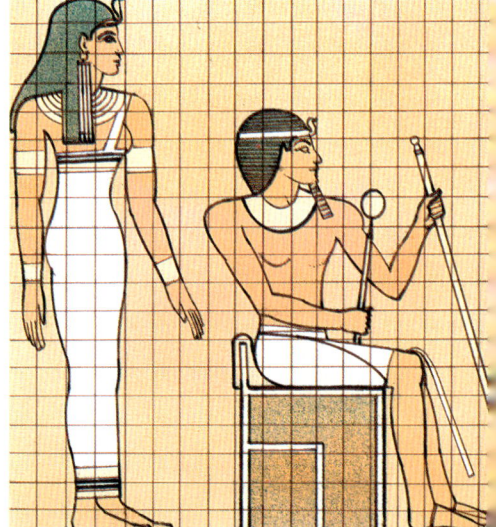

An unequal conflict

The Egyptian army, with 20 thousand men and only 50 war chariots, was divided into 4 divisions (Amon, Re', Ptah, and Seth). The Hittites, under the command of King Muwatallis II, had 16 thousand men and 2,500 war chariots. The Egyptians probably had a narrow victory, but the event was celebrated as a triumph.

Bronze weapons
Unlike the Hittites, iron and its uses were unknown to the Egyptians. The Egyptian dagger and short scimitar were made of bronze with damask handles.

Ramses II
Ramses II leads the Amon division driving his war chariot, pulled by plumed horses. He wears the War Crown, but does not even wear light armor, to show his disregard for the enemy.

Conflict with the Hittites

Under the Nineteenth Dynasty, the Egyptians measured their power against that of the Hittites, an Indo-European people who invented iron weapons, and had settled in Anatolia during the seventeenth century B.C. Already during the reign of Amenhotep IV, the Hittites had sent military expeditions into the Levant as far as Lebanon to profit from Egypt's temporary religious troubles. First, Seti I fought them. Then, the task fell to Ramses II, who crushed them at Kadesh, on the river Orontes, around 1299 B.C. A treaty of perpetual peace between Ramses II and Hattusilis III of the Hittites followed, marked by the marriage between the pharaoh and the daughter of Hattusilis III.

The Sea Peoples

For both empires, a new threat appeared: the invasion of the Sea Peoples. The Sea Peoples were a confederation of tribes whose names reveal their Mediterranean origins. The Sea Peoples, confidant of their striking power, migrated with their wives and children in search of rich territories. About 1200 B.C., they caused the fall of the Hittite Empire. Afterwards, the Delta attracted their attention. Ramses III of the Twentieth Dynasty, the last great sovereign of Egypt, conclusively repelled them in 1190 B.C.

Ramses III
The great battle led by Ramses III against the landing of the Sea Peoples in the big relief of the funerary temple of the pharaoh at Medinet Habu (west of Thebes).

Troops and armies

Professional soldiers formed the armies that defeated the Hittites and disbanded the Sea Peoples. They descended from family lines of warriors. Periodically, the army scribe enrolled new recruits that were trained for military careers by exacting instructors. They were "national" armies bureaucratically organized like the civil administration. The army's superior chief was the pharaoh. Under him, in order, was the "great general," then various lesser generals, and finally plenty of captains and ensigns commanding platoons. The ensigns carried the banners of the battalions, which echoed the totemic emblems of the old provinces. Men were organized in divisions, which included infantry—armed with daggers and spears and protected with leather shields, leather helmets, and linen armor—and also chariot troops. The charioteers rode light, fast wooden war chariots with some parts made from leather or metal elements, as well as radial wheels; they were pulled by two horses (the Hittites had taught them an unforgettable lesson). There were also archers and several special combat troops with axes, shields, and boomerangs. The king had a short scimitar, a leather apron covered with metal scales, and a metal helmet, called a "blue crown." The omnipresent scribes were also part of the regular army. Quartermasters were in charge of administration and provisions, trumpeters transmitted orders, and dispatch riders were the scribes' subordinates. The troops not only could depend upon receiving their wages, but also on receiving their share of the division of the spoils and rich rewards. Honorary decorations consisted of heavy gold necklaces and bracelets. The most desired ones were the "flies," jewels that gave so much prestige as to transcend their precious value. Sometimes, men and women enemy prisoners were

THE BATTLE OF KADESH
1299 B.C.

First phase
The Hittite chariots attack the flank, crushing the Re' division. The survivors, pursued by enemies, tried to reach the Amon (1) division and Ramses' camp. The Ptah and Seth divisions (2) are still far away.

Second phase
The Egyptians regroup themselves. They counterattack and scatter the enemy, who is strangled by the arrival of the Ptah (3) division. The Hittite infantry and the Seth division did not participate in the battle (4).

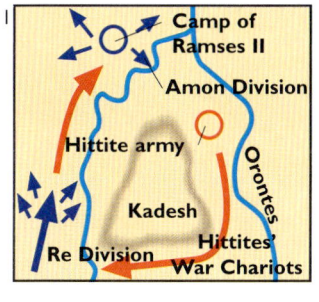

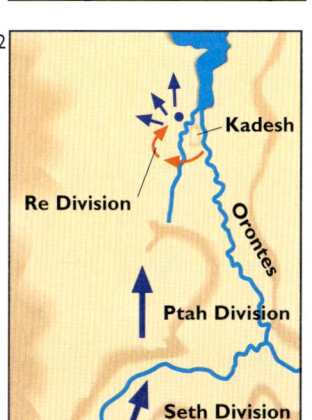

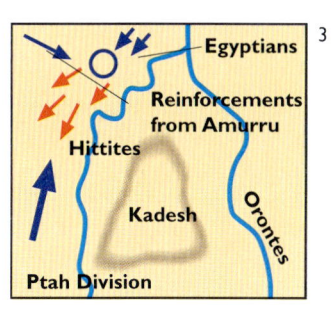

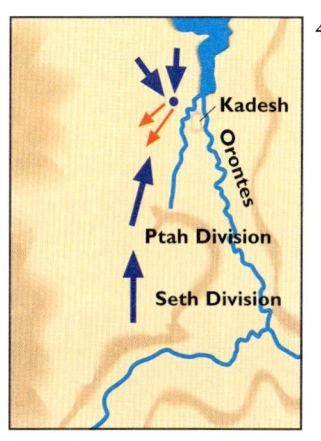

Tactics and formations
The battle of Kadesh is the first battle in history whose tactics and formations are known.

111

left as slaves to those who had captured them, but, in general, they were fully integrated into society and considered subjects of the pharaoh. Usually, battles finished in big clashes where not only dexterity and personal training counted, but discipline and quick moves were required on the part of the officers.

Abu Simbel

The military operations in Syria and Palestine did not cause the pharaohs to neglect the southern territories, especially Nubia, which, since the Middle Kingdom, had come under Egypt's direct control. This region was a cushion area along the southern border and, more importantly, possessed remarkable mines of gold and other minerals as well as timber. Moreover, Nubian warriors enlisted in the Egyptian armies.

Abu Simbel was the door to Lower Nubia, which stretched up to the fortresses close by the Second Cataract. The city had a high strategic role. It was built behind one of the few craggy areas of Egypt and, since the pyramidal ages, had been the center that controlled all the stone quarries that formed the blocks before loading them onto the barges that descended the Nile. Its harbor had remained active during the Middle Kingdom and welcomed the armies sent to conquer the south and sent provisions to them. The quarries and harbor remained efficient, even during the New Kingdom when, under Ramses II, yards for the huge rocky temples were opened.

The colossi
The four monumental sculptures of the sanctuary represented the great god of the three main Egyptian centers. They are Ptah, from Memphis; Amon, from Thebes; and Re from Heliopolis. The third from the left is Ramses II, autodeified during his lifetime.

The minor temple
A smaller temple honored Hathor, goddess of love, music, and dance, and Queen Nefertari, wife of Ramses II. The facade displays four statues of the King and two of the Queen.

High tech
In the 1960s, a dam, known as the *High Dam*, barred the Nile near Aswan, creating Lake Nasser. To prevent the waters from submerging the Abu Simbel temples, they have been dismantled and rebuilt 689 ft. farther back and 2,145 ft. higher than their original site. The work lasted 10 years (1963-1972).

THE CHISELED MOUNTAIN
Carvers and stonecutters sculpt the four colossi in the cliffs. In the rocky temple of Ramses II at Abu Simbel, they act as pillars of local temples.

THE DECLINE OF EGYPT

The Hittites' warfare marked the beginning of the Iron Age in Egypt, a period that saw the total disruption of the country and its subjugation to foreign invaders. The new rulers followed the tradition of the pharaohs.

Under the successors of Ramses III, the Asian territories were lost, and misery and disorder wracked the country. The royal authority was weakened so much that the high priest of Thebes overpowered the pharaoh. This was the Third Intermediate period (1085–322), during which the country was governed by dynasties of foreign origins, one Libyan and another Nubian. In 671 B.C., Egypt was invaded and conquered by the Assyrians who, during the fall of the Hittites, had imposed their leadership in the Near East. Independence was regained one last time by the Twenty-sixth Dynasty founded by Psammetichus I, but for no more than a century (672–525 B.C.). He chose Sais as the new capital on the Delta (the Saite Dynasty). A vigorous commerce with

The invasions
A map of the invasions that Egypt has endured during the last 700 years.

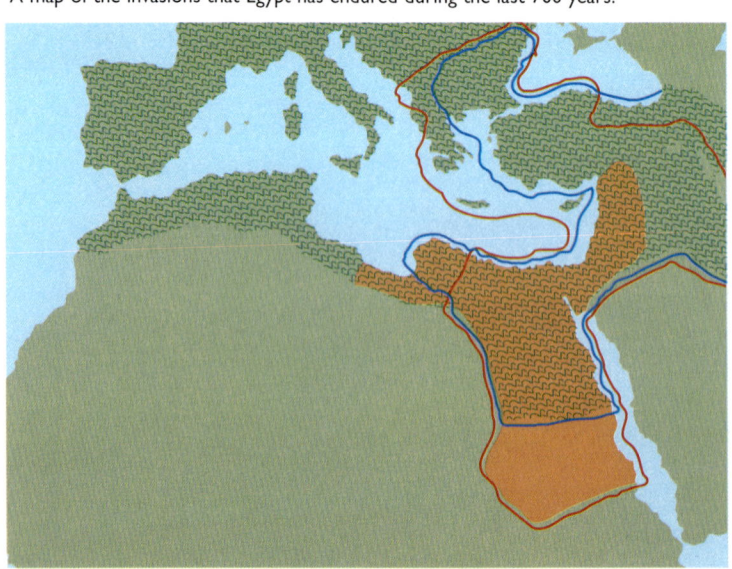

Thrace, Greece, and maximum expansion of the Empire of Alexander the Great

Maximum expansion of the Persian Empire

The Egyptian Empire

Maximum expansion of the Roman Empire

Alexander the Great
Undoubtedly, the most spectacular warrior of the antiquity, he seized Egypt and all the Persian Empire from King Darius III.

The same rituals
Even under Roman domination, the Egyptians remained faithful to their funerary rites. In addition to a pasteboard of mummy, this plastered and decorated shell covered the corpse of the deceased.

The same gods
Foreign domination did not expel the traditional gods from their pantheon. In this stele of the Saite Dynasty, Osiris welcomes a dead person.

the Greeks began and Egypt was again at its prime. However, an adequate military force did not support the renewed prosperity. So in 525 B.C., Egypt fell under the power of the Persians, becoming a simple province of their empire. Things changed when Alexander the Great conquered Egypt during his expedition against Persia in 332 B.C.), crowning himself pharaoh.

Hellenistic Egypt

Among the many towns that Alexander the Great had conquered and renamed with his own name, there was one in Egypt, founded on the westernmost mouth of the Nile. At Alexander's death in 323 B.C., his vast empire was parceled out among his generals. Egypt passed to Ptolemy, forerunner of a new dynasty known as Ptolemaic Dynasty, as all his successors chose his name.

Under the Ptolemaic Dynasty, the capital Alexandria became the major cultural and commercial center of late antiquity, heir of the classical Greek culture. Ptolemy II, ruling from 285 to 246 B.C., opened the Museum ("place of the Muses"). It was similar to a modern university, with an enormous library, which covered all the subjects of science. The cultural patrimony of more than three centuries (from the third century B.C. to the first century A.D.) was called Alexandrine (from the city of Alexandria) or Hellenistic (from *Hellas* or Greece). The Ptolemies ruled Egypt undisturbed until 47 B.C., when Julius Caesar reduced Egypt to a subject province of Rome, with Cleopatra, sister of the last Ptolemy (the thir-

Ptolemy II
Cameo reproducing the profile of Ptolemy II, called *Philadelphus* ("sister-loving"), and that of his wife and sister Arsinoe.

The Nile
Hellenistic art represents the Nile as an old man holding ears of corn with generations of children at his feet.

THE LIBRARY OF ALEXANDRIA
The most brilliant scholars of the time came from the Mediterranean regions to study its 700,000 volumes.

The Grand Tour
Cairo's Islamic monuments as seen by a European artist of the 19th century, when Egypt was a favorite resort of travelers.

The Nile seen by the Romans
The Nile and its floods in a Roman mosaic in the *Tempio della Fortuna Primigenia* at Palestrina

The flight into Egypt
The Gospel episode in a fresco by Giotto at the basilica of Assisi in Italy.

New themes
Since the 4th century A.D., Egyptian art took its themes from the Christian tradition.

Fabric of the 7th century, representing a military saint amid imaginary characters.

teenth) on the throne. From 30 B.C. to A.D. 642, Egypt remained a Roman province. When the Roman emperor Theodosius I split the empire into two halves, the Western and the Eastern, the rich country of the Nile was ruled from the eastern capital, Constantinople.

Egypt, a Christian and Islamic land

In Egypt, tradition claims that St. Mark founded the first church in Alexandria. From that time on, the new religion planted its seeds deeply thanks to saints like St. Anthony, the great hermit of the third century. Monasticism was born in Egypt. Later on, it grew into communities under the direction of St. Pachomios. In the fifth century, doctrinal antagonisms arose among the Christians of Egypt. On one side were the native Egyptians, the Copts, and on the other the Melkites, who accepted the leadership of Constantinople. The final rupture came after the Council of Chalcedon in A.D. 451. The Copts held that in Jesus there was but a single divine nature, while the Melkites believed that he also held a complete human nature. Coptic doctrine remained firmly rooted in the whole country. It did not disappear even when Egypt was conquered by the Arabs in A.D. 642 and became part of the Islam world.

With the Arabs, a new historical phase began, that of medieval Egypt. After a brief pause, the country reemerged again, assuming the role of a leading guide of the Arab world. Cairo, pulsing with life, became its center.

INDEX

A

Abu Simbel 84, 85, 112, 113
Abydos 65
Aegean Sea 70
Africa 8
Ahmose 83
Akhenaten 100
Akhet 20, 21
Alexander the Great 11, 114, 115
Alexandria 5, 14, 15, 115, 116, 117, 119
  Library 116, 117
  Museum 116
Amenemhet III 71
Amenhotep II 87
Amenhotep III 87, 95, 104
Amenhotep IV 87, 100, 101, 109
Amenhotep V (Akhenaten) 85
Amon 70, 88, 94, 95, 100–103, 108, 111
Anatolia 107
Ankh (cross) 90
Anubis 55
Arsinoe 116
Asia 8, 81, 86
  Minor 84
Assisi 119
Aswan 12, 13, 15, 16, 30, 58, 65, 113
Asyut 12
Atbara (river) 12
Aten 100, 101
Atum 51, 52
Avaris 14, 15, 82

B

Bahr Yusef 12, 74
Battle of Kadesh 111
Belgium 14
Bible 7
Byblos 31, 70
Byzantium (Constantinople) 119

C

Cairo (Memphis) 7, 12, 13, 15, 59, 118, 119
  Museum 63
Canopic jars 54, 103
Carnavon, George, Lord 7
Carter, Howard 7, 102
Champollion, Jean-François 7
Charter of the Six, the 35
Colossi of Memnon, monolithic statues 95, 104
Concilium of Nicea 119
Crete 70, 72, 87
Cyprus 87

D

Dhashur 32, 60
Damietta 12
Darius III, the Great 115
Deir el-Bahri 87
Deir el-Medina 104–106
Denon, Dominique-Vivant 7
Description de l'Égypte, treatise by V. Denon 7, 62

E

Edfu 64
Ennead 51, 52
Euphrates River (the) 87
Europe 7

F

Faiyum 10, 12, 13, 68, 70, 73, 74, 75, 76
France 7

G

Geb 51, 52
Giotto 119
Giza 31, 32, 56, 59, 60
Gospels 119
Greece 114, 116

H

Hapi 17, 20
Harmakhis 62
Harper's Song (the), an ancient lyrical Egyptian composition 66, 98
Hathor 36, 53, 87, 92
Hatshepsut 86, 87, 97
Heliopolis 31, 51, 52
Heracleopolis 64
Hermopolis 52
Herodotus 5, 6, 16, 58, 59
Hieroglyphs 7, 43, 44, 45
Horn of Africa 32
Horus 11, 36, 37, 53, 62, 64

Hyksos 15, 81–84, 111

I

Imhotep 44, 56
Instruction of the Vizier Ptahhotep, a Wisdom book 98
Isis 5, 20, 51–54, 87
Israelites 83

J

Julius Caesar 116

K

Ka 50, 94, 96, 97
Kadesh 111
Kamose 83
Karnak 88, 94, 95
Kemet 14
Kerma 78
Khafre 36, 57, 59, 62
Khartoum 12, 78
Khast 14
Khepri 52
Kheti III 65
Khnum 53
Khonsu 53
Khufu 57, 58–61

L

Lebanon 107
Luxor (Thebes) 15, 88, 95

M

Ma'at 11, 30, 37–40
Mariette, Auguste 7, 62
Mastaba 56, 60
Medinet Habu 110
Mediterranean Sea 6, 12, 14, 15, 16, 68, 72, 84
Megiddo 86
Memphis 14, 15, 31, 32, 33, 52, 65, 68, 69, 119
Menes 11
Menkaure 56, 59
Mentuhotep I 65
Mentuhotep II 65, 66, 68
Mesopotamia 84, 93
Mirgissa 78
Moeris, Lake 75
Mummy 4, 115

N

Napoleon Bonaparte 5, 6, 7, 62
Naquada I 9, 10
Naquada II 10
Narmer 10, 11
Narmer's Palette, a votive tablet 10, 34
Nasser, Lake 78, 113
Natron 55, 96
Nefertari 113
Nefertiti 85, 101
Nefertum 52
Nefret 38
Nephthys 51, 52, 53
Neith 52
Nekhbet 37
Nile 8–10, 12–16, 18, 19–21, 23, 24, 28, 29, 31, 33, 49, 64, 65, 74, 78, 82, 85, 88, 102, 103, 112, 113, 116, 118, 119

Nubia 12, 30, 31, 32, 70, 78, 84, 101, 102, 112, 119
Nut 51, 52, 76, 78

O

Obelisk 4
Ogdoad 52
Osiris 5, 20, 50–52, 54, 115

P

Palermo Stone (the) 30
Palestine 6, 101, 112
Palestrina 118
Papyrus 11, 22, 24, 26, 43, 44, 71, 106
Ebers Medical Papyrus, text of medicine 98
Pepi I 30, 35
Pepi II 64
Peret 20, 21, 24, 26
Persia 115
Pharaoh 4, 7, 30–32, 34–39, 41, 42, 44, 45, 48, 52, 54, 58, 62–65, 68, 70–73, 87, 88, 90, 91, 93, 97, 103, 110–115
Phoenicia 31, 87, 93
Plutarch 5
Psammetichus I 114
Ptah 32, 52, 112
Ptolemy 7, 116
Ptolemy II, Philadelphus 116
Ptolemy V 7
Ptolemy XIV 116
Punt 32
Pyramid 4, 32, 35, 40, 44, 46, 56–62, 78, 88
of Giza 56, 57

of Khafre 57, 59, 60
of Khufu (the Great Pyramid) 57, 59–61
of Menkaure 56
of Snefru 32, 60
of Zoser 60
Pyramid Texts, a hymn 14

R

Rahotep 38
Ramesseum, the (funerary temple) 85, 103
Ramses II 84, 85, 94, 101, 112, 113
Ramses III 101, 110, 111, 114
Re 37, 52, 53, 112
Red Sea 15, 32, 65
Rekhmire 34
Rosetta 5, 6, 7, 12
Rosetta Stone (the) 5

S

Sahara 8, 9
Sahure 32
Saint Anthony 119
Sais 14, 15, 114
Saqqara 31, 32, 44, 46, 56, 60
Satire of the Trades (the), ancient Egyptian text 42, 45, 98
Scribe 36, 39, 41–44, 46, 72, 81, 99, 106, 111

Sekhmet 52
Semma 78
Sesostris I 71, 79
Sesostris III 70, 74
Seth 20, 51, 52, 54
Seti I 87
Shemu 20, 21, 26
Shu 51, 52
Sinai 31, 80
Sirius (Sothis) 17, 20
Snefru 32, 57, 60
Sobek 52, 75
Sphinx 62, 63, 95
Stele of King Snake 11
Story of Sinuhe 98
Submission of a prisoner, a tomb fresco 41
Sudan 12
Suez 70
Syria 112

T

Tefnut 51, 52
Tell el-Amarna 85, 101
Temple/Temples 5, 38, 40, 43, 78, 85, 87, 88, 91, 93, 94–99, 110, 113
of Queen Hatshepsut 103
Thebes 15, 64, 65, 68, 74, 83, 85, 88, 90, 94, 95, 100, 101, 110, 114
Theodosius 5, 119
Thinis 15, 31

Thrace 114
Thutmose I 84, 103
Thutmose II 84
Thutmose III 86, 87, 93
Thutmose IV 41, 63, 86
Tomb of Iti 67
of Sennedjem 16
Tura 57, 103
Tutankhamen 7, 102, 103

U

Uronarti 78
Uto 37

V

Valley of the Kings (the) 102–104
Valley of the Queens (the) 104
Vizier 36–38, 44

W

Wadi Halfa 78, 79

Z

Zedefra 62
Zoser 32, 44, 56, 60

Acknowledgments

The illustrations displayed in this volume are new and original. They have been realized upon a project by DoGi s.p.a. that owns its copyright.

ILLLUSTRATIONS:
Bartolozzi: 13, 14–15, 32–33, 68–69, 84–85; Gaudenzi: 15c, 112–113; Ranchetti: 7t, 11c, 20t, 21b, 35, 45t, 78b, 94–95b, 111, 114b; Saraceni: 4–5, 6t, 10t, 44b, 51, 52–53, 60–61, 110t, 115t; Sergio: 6–7, 8–9, 18–19, 20–21, 22–23, 24–25, 26–27, 28–29, 42, 43, 48–49, 58–59, 72–73, 74–75, 76–77, 78, 79, 80–81, 82–83, 88–89, 90–91, 92–93, 96–97, 98–99, 100t, 102–103, 104t, 104–105, 106, 107, 108–109, 117; Studio Inklink: 34b, 54–55.

REPRODUCTIONS AND DOCUMENTS:
DoGi s.p.a. has done its best to discover possible rights of third parties. We apologize for any omissions or mistakes that might have occurred, and we will be pleased to introduce the appropriate corrections in the later editions of this book.
Alinari/Giradon: 113l; DoGi Archives: 4, 13t, 47br, 62t, 66l, 70, 84b, 85t, 110, 116t, 118t, 118b, 119b; DoGi Archives/Mario Quattrone: 119t; DoGi Archives/Sandro Scalia: 30br; Ashmolean Museum: 10b; Contrasto Agency: 14, 58-59; Contrasto Agency/E. Lessing: 100; Contrasto Agency/Magnum Photo/E. Lessing: 40, 41c, 47c, 53r, 64, 66–67, 67r, 87c, 92, 95b, 101l, 101r, 102; British Museum: 7, 54b; Vatican Museum: 116b; Siliotti: 9, 10t, 11, 12, 13c, 13b, 16–17, 30t, 30bl, 31, 34, 36t, 36b, 37, 38–39, 39t, 41b, 42–43, 44, 45, 46, 47b, 50, 53l, 59, 62b, 63, 65, 71t, 71r, 85b, 86, 87r, 90, 95t, 103t, 103b, 105, 109, 115c, 115t.
COVER: Studio Inklink
FRONTISPIECE: Sergio
ABBREVIATIONS: *t: top/ b: below/ c: center/ r: right/ l: left*